THE ALL-AMERICAN MUSCLE CAR

THE RISE, FALL AND RESURRECTION of DETROIT'S GREATEST PERFORMANCE CARS

JOE OLDHAM | JIM WANGERS | COLIN COMER
DAVID NEWHARDT | RANDY LEFFINGWELL

EDITED BY DARWIN HOLMSTROM

motorbooks

Quarto is the authority on a wide range of topics.
Quarto educates, entertains and enriches the lives of
our readers—enthusiasts and lovers of hands-on living.
www.quartoknows.com

First published in 2013 by Motorbooks, an imprint of
The Quarto Group, 401 Second Avenue North, Suite 310,
Minneapolis, MN 55401 USA. Telephone: (612) 344-8100
Fax: (612) 344-8692

quartoknows.com
Visit our blogs at quartoknows.com

Motorbooks titles are also available at discount for retail,
wholesale, promotional, and bulk purchase. For details, contact
the Special Sales Manager by email at specialsales@quarto.com
or by mail at The Quarto Group, Attn: Special Sales Manager,
401 Second Avenue North, Suite 310, Minneapolis, MN 55401
USA.

10 9 8 7 6 5 4 3 2 1

ISBN: 978-0-7603-5335-6

The Library of Congress has cataloged the hardcover edition of
this book as follows:

Wangers, Jim.
 The all-American muscle car : the birth, death and
resurrection of Detroit's greatest performance cars /
by Jim Wangers and Colin Comer.
  pages cm
 ISBN 978-0-7603-4382-1 (hardcover)
 1. Muscle cars--United States--History. I. Comer, Colin. II.
Title.
 TL23.W285 2013
 629.222--dc23
                                2012049180

Acquiring Editor: Darwin Holmstrom
Layout: Brad Norr Design

On the front cover: Plymouth Road Runner 1971.
 Archives/TEN: The Enthusiasts Magazines, LLC.
On the back cover: Ford ignited the twenty-first-century
muscle-car wars with its all-new 2004 Mustang GT.
On the title page: 1969 Dodge Daytona Charger

Printed in China

MIX
Paper from
responsible sources
FSC® C016973

CONTENTS

Introduction: Real Muscle Cars

Darwin Holmstrom

When John Z. DeLorean and his cadre of enthusiastic miscreants took it upon themselves to bolt Pontiac division's hottest engine into a mid-sized chassis, disobeying orders from the top of General Motors' food chain, they created something that should never have been and will never be again: the muscle car.

The time was right for anything that symbolized a raised middle finger thrust at society. The Rolling Stones were recording their first album, a collection of horny American blues songs that were considered far too "negro" to be played on American radio. Ken Kesey made preparations to hit the road in his psychedelic bus *Further* and bring his acid tests, parties in which participants were dosed with LSD-25 and tripped balls, from San Francisco to the entire nation, and Huey Newton and Bobby Seale were laying the foundation for what would become the Black Panther Party. In retrospect, the muscle car seemed relatively harmless.

But not to the suits running General Motors, a company that found itself under assault on two fronts. First, the Automobile Manufacturer's Association (AMA) still enforced a strict ban on its members participating in racing. This ban proved to be symbolic, since the AMA had no teeth which with to enforce it, and both Ford and Chrysler openly defied the ban whenever it suited their corporate purposes, but not GM. That was because of reason number two: the federal government was threatening to break up GM because the company's overall share of the auto market was so large that it was on the verge of becoming an illegal monopoly, according the antitrust laws of the day. This was no idle threat; the U.S. government had broken up Standard Oil a half century earlier for the very same reason. Thus GM obeyed the AMA ban not because of some sort of

There are muscle cars, and then there are *muscle cars*. The one-of-a-kind Shelby Super Snake was the most muscular of the breed.

devotion to good citizenship, but rather because the company had nothing to gain from the publicity that racing attracted.

Either way, GM was not receptive to the innovations that DeLorean and his own band of merry pranksters were about to unleash on the automotive scene, so they had to bring the results of their off-hours engineering exercises—the Pontiac GTO—to market through the back door, offering the GTO as an option package on the Pontiac Tempest.

What the cadavers occupying the top floors of GM's corporate headquarters failed to grasp, the motoring public bought in droves. The GTO was a huge success, as were its successors like the Ford Mustang, the Dodge Charger, and the Chevrolet Camaro. The GTO anticipated a new breed of performance car aimed at a new breed of buyer: the Baby Boom generation, tens of millions of young buyers entering the auto market each year. And no car company, not even mild-mannered American Motors Corporation, builders of the humble Rambler

economy cars, could afford to ignore this vast, affluent, and hungry market.

The classic muscle car era, which began when the first Pontiac buyer checked the GTO box on the Pontiac Tempest option order list and ended when the last Super Duty 455 Firebird rolled off Pontiac's assembly line in 1974, was something that should have never been. In hindsight, who can legitimately argue that giving teenage boys lightweight cars stuffed full of big-block V-8 power, crude handling abilities for harnessing that power, and virtually no braking power to bring the festivities to a halt once everything went south, which it did more often than not, was a good idea?

Even though building these cars for kids was unwise, like giving heroin to Keith Richards or a race car to James Dean or Marilyn Monroe to a horny president, the resulting cars were pretty damned cool. The cars might have been overpowered, poor-handling death traps, but unless a person has driven one of these outrageous machines, he or she has never really lived. The muscle car was something that should never have been, but those of us who love them are damned glad they existed.

Likewise the muscle car is something that never will be again. Sure, we have cars today that will outperform the classic muscle cars in every measurable way. We have faster cars. We have better handling cars. We have more comfortable cars. We have safer cars. We have cars that can run through the quarter mile fifty percent quicker than cars of the classic era. We have cars that will halve the time a classic muscle car took to get through a slalom course. We have cars that will do all this while coddling the driver in as much comfort as he or she would find in the luxury suite of a five-star hotel and keeping him or her as safe as it is possible to be in a moving vehicle. These are wonderful cars, but they are not the same. They do not raise their middle fingers in a rousing "fuck-you" salute to authority the way real muscle cars do. Real muscle cars don't have nineteen airbags. Real muscle cars don't have traction control. Real muscle cars don't even have power steering or air conditioning. Instead they have big engines for people with big enough clackers to use them. And that's about it.

What more do you need?

1

GTO: The Birth of the Muscle Car

Jim Wangers

It was a Saturday morning in the early spring of 1963. In the Pontiac Garage at the GM Proving Grounds, suspended high on a lift, was Pontiac's 1964 model year intermediate A-body Tempest, powered by a 326-cubic-inch V-8 engine. John DeLorean, Pontiac Chief Engineer, and two of his senior assistants, Bill Collins and Russ Gee, gazed up at the car. As engineers are prone to do, they scanned the vehicle, pondering the "what ifs" in the never-ending pursuit of improving on what is there, or making something altogether new from what they had. It was this inauspicious moment that the idea of the Pontiac GTO was born.

Preface

I often say, "I am lucky to have been in the right place at the right time" when asked about my involvement at Pontiac, in particular with the GTO. I am grateful to the Pontiac community for anointing me the affectionate title of the "Godfather of the GTO." Having had the honor bestowed upon me, countless folks inquire as to how I invented this early muscle car. I actually had very little to do with the development of the product that would eventually be known as the Pontiac GTO—that credit goes to John DeLorean, Bill Collins, and Russ Gee.

Before I get too far ahead of myself, it is only fair to share with you how Pontiac became positioned to make the extraordinary move to the forefront of an era we know and love—the era of the American muscle car.

Once the auto industry retooled after World War II, a new taste for styling and performance began to evolve. Rather than view their cars only as utilities, consumers now looked at their cars as extensions of themselves. Known as only a "good reliable"

Every Pontiac featured the famous split-grille front end, but when you read the letters *GTO*, you knew you were looking at something special. With the exception of the 1974 model year, this emblem was always mounted on the driver's side of the twin-grille assembly.

car, Pontiac had fallen to the bottom in the sales race among all the General Motors Divisions by the mid-1950s. As a new generation was entering the market, they wanted more than just a nice dependable car; they wanted style and performance. Though Pontiac introduced their 1955 model year body style with a revolutionary new OHV V-8, the public did not take to the car. In fact, Pontiac was seen as simply a "big Chevy"! In 1956, with sales still floundering, General Motors' management had a serious decision to make—kill the division or find new blood to run it.

Bunkie Knudsen & Performance

General Motors needed to make a change! In an unpopular move, Harlow Curtis, then president of GM, appointed a young Semon E. "Bunkie" Knudsen as the new general manager of Pontiac. Bunkie was given the mission of turning the division around within five years, or the corporation would kill it!

Back then, a division general manager was powerful, responsible for all elements of his division, calling all the shots. Knudsen had very little sales experience, which made his appointment something of a head scratcher for other GM employees. Critics were certain he got the job solely because his father was a former president

of GM. It was, in fact, truly ironic. As a young sales executive, Curtis had been tapped by the elder Knudsen to take over a floundering Buick division in the mid-1930s. He turned Buick around, and now, twenty years later as the current GM President, Curtis remembered the opportunity he had been given by Knudsen's father. He selected young Bunkie Knudsen to resurrect Pontiac—and in doing so, set the young Knudsen upon the same path that Knudsen's father had charted for him.

Curtis also appointed his old friend Frank Bridge to take over as general sales manager at Pontiac. Bridge had been an assistant sales manager at Buick,

and he knew how to "move iron" into the hands of consumers. Bridge, unfortunately, had little understanding of marketing, which I later learned made our efforts to establish a performance image irrelevant as far as he was concerned.

The first thing Knudsen did when he arrived at Pontiac was to come to grips with its boring image—a serious problem that he knew had the division virtually headed for extinction. Knudsen was a good manufacturing guy and a bit of a racer himself. An initial move he made that proved more symbolic than functional was to remove the famed Silver Streaks, a pair of chrome strips that had adorned Pontiac hoods and

Every stick-shift GTO came with standard bucket seats. A bench seat was a no-cost option. Manually shifted cars also came with a floor-mounted Hurst shifter, with or without the optional console. Many **serious racers chose to pass on the console to save weight, but few real enthusiasts could pass up the factory gauge package or wood-style steering wheel.**

rear decks since the thirties. This was a strong statement from the new guy in charge, showing that he understood the sacrifices Pontiac would have to make in order to remain competitive. He then challenged his team of engineers to build more horsepower and performance into the car. He was going to turn "grandma into a teenager," to coin one of his favorite maxims. He was going to make the unsexy sexy and the slow fast. He meant to change Pontiac forever.

With Knudsen's performance mantra now in place, word spread around Detroit about what was happening at Pontiac. As a young product enthusiast, I approached Pontiac and Knudsen. "This is where I want to work," I told them. I was referred to the advertising agency, and luckily, I was in the right place at the right time. The agency really needed a product guy, and I soon found myself working for MacManus, John & Adams exclusively on the Pontiac account.

Knudsen next recruited Elliot M. "Pete" Estes away from Oldsmobile, where he had been an assistant chief engineer, to become Pontiac's new chief engineer. Knudsen and Estes worked very well together as a team. One of the smartest early moves they made was to hire a very talented young engineer who had become available after the collapse of Packard. His name was John DeLorean, a name that would ultimately become indelibly imprinted in Pontiac history. The trio of Knudsen, Estes, and DeLorean went on to build more than a decade of some of the most exciting and successful new cars the U.S. auto industry had ever seen, and I was so lucky to be a part of it.

Author Jim Wangers takes the original *Car and Driver* test car for a spin around the world-famous Bob's Big Boy restaurant in Toluca Lake, California. This beautifully restored masterpiece is owned by Tenney Fairchild.

How to tell a real tiger from a pussycat:

Drive it.

Pontiac Motor Division • General Motors Corporation

Two seconds behind the wheel of a Pontiac and you know unquestionably you're in tiger country. You realize right away there's more to being a tiger than just bucket seats, carpeting, and sleek upholstery. There's Wide-Track handling, say. And availability of a six or two rambunctious V-8s in the LeMans. And a snarling 335-hp GTO or its 360-hp, slightly hairier, cousin. Get out and drive a tiger!

**Quick Wide-Track Tigers
Pontiac LeMans & GTO**

As a real racing enthusiast, Knudsen had befriended many famous racers and race-car builders, men like Mickey Thompson, Ray Nichels, and Smoky Yunick, all young and all "comers" in their field. Knudsen was going racing, determined to win and make a bold statement. Pontiac first showed up at Daytona Beach in 1957. With Nichels organizing the effort, names like John Zink Jr., John Littlejohn, and Cotton Owens raced Pontiac into virtual dominance at the midwinter Daytona Beach Speed Week activity.

Early performance efforts were underscored with parts designed in the automotive aftermarket. Knudsen wanted these parts to be engineered in-house, and he soon created the Super Duty Group within his own engineering department. Early members of the group included Malcolm "Mac" MacKeller, engine specialist

Russ Gee, and chassis engineer Bill Collins. Managing the group was Bill Klinger, while Frank Barnard handled parts distribution. Many parts engineered, designed, and produced during that period are still in use today.

Pontiac did not only become successful in stock car racing. The Super Duty Package also made Pontiac a serious contender on the drag strip as well, so well that other drivers almost gave up. The joke around NASCAR at the time was, "It will be a good race if those damn Pontiacs don't show up!"

Besides winning on the track, Pontiac was winning in the showroom too. Dealers were happy. The product line seemed endless. The Bonneville, first introduced only as a convertible in 1957, was now Pontiac's luxury leader, while the Grand Prix and Catalina models were available with an endless variety of options to suit just about every buyer's desire.

Having been on the verge of ruin less than ten years earlier, Pontiac was now solidly performing at number three in the auto sales race, surpassed only by Chevrolet and Ford. Knudsen's vision of creating a performance image proved to be a winning formula that dealers were quickly leveraging into sales.

The heart and soul of any Pontiac given the Royal Bobcat treatment was the Tri-Power 389.

The Royal Bobcat's long and low look was a trademark of all the wide-track Pontiacs of the era.

GM itself was soaring with a market share that had grown to more than 55 percent in 1966, a fact hard to believe in today's time. All was grand until the government stepped in. GM's market share was viewed to be too dominant, so the Justice Department threatened to take action to break up the corporation should they ever get close to a 60 percent market share.

The corporation's reaction was to kill all racing activity. A memo was issued to all divisions in January 1963 to discontinue immediately all factory support of organized motorsports. They even appointed a well-known cheater who knew how to slip parts out the back door—Ed Cole, then a Chevrolet engineer—to monitor compliance. Who better to catch a cheat than a cheater?

We had been using Pontiac's success on the racetrack to subtly convey the car's benefits in our Wide-Track advertising campaign. We were really making strides building our new image. The racing ban would now take us off our stage, potentially curbing this new popularity Pontiac had worked hard to gain.

Our concern soon disappeared, however, thanks to an absolutely genius move—Pontiac resolved to take the success of racing off the track and put it on the street!

When he wasn't marketing Pontiacs, Wangers was racing them and winning national championships in the process.

GTO Birth Moment

Over the years, there have been quite a few incredible misrepresentations of just how the famous car came about. In spite of my ongoing attempts to set the record straight, I am still credited with having made too many contributions to the actual development of the car itself. I did not submit the idea of stuffing a 389-cubic-inch engine into the new intermediate A-body. My role was to sell it, and with that, as some folks say, I created the mystique that surrounds the GTO even today.

Wangers' race cars used a pair of four-barrel carburetors in place of the three two-barrel setup on the street cars.

Here is how the car actually was created. It took place one Saturday morning at the GM Proving Grounds in Milford, Michigan. As chief engineer, John DeLorean was keen on planned *what if?* sessions that took place on Saturday mornings. He would invite members of his engineering staff and a select group of other important folks to come out to Milford for a day of reviewing new ideas and driving new cars. One day in the spring of 1963, a prototype 1964 Tempest Coupe equipped with a 326-cubic-inch engine was up on a lift. DeLorean and two of his favorite engineers, Russ Gee and Bill Collins, were under the car scrutinizing the chassis.

While looking up, Collins casually mentioned, "You know, John, with the engine mounts being the same, it would take us about twenty minutes to slip a 389 into this thing." DeLorean caught an approving nod from Gee, and without uttering a word, the three were all in agreement.

One week later, the assembled Saturday morning group was greeted by another prototype 1964 Tempest Coupe. This particular Tempest housed a 389-cubic-inch engine. It had a four-barrel carburetor and was backed by a four-speed Muncie transmission and a limited slip rear end. Those privileged to drive this prototype that morning were blown away—while nobody specifically mentioned it, they all knew that this 389-cubic-inch-powered A-body would put Pontiac in a performance class of its own, way above fellow divisions Chevy, Oldsmobile, and Buick.

The 389-cubic-inch engine was exactly what the 3,500-pound new Tempest needed. The engine had plenty of low-end torque and lots of mid-range horsepower. With each new change, the prototype got better and better. They added additional suspension tuning, a heavier clutch, and looked at a different tire. DeLorean made the car his personal driver and on several occasions loaned it to close friends. He always had a hard time getting it back.

As to the name, that was all DeLorean. Ferrari was using the term "GTO" for one of their new

The on-track success of the Royal Bobcats did much to enhance their reputation on the street.

The 1964 GTO was not only a sales success; it completely reshaped a
generation's expectations of what a performance car could be.

GTO is for kicking up the kind of storm that others just talk up.

Standard Equipment: engine: 389-cu. in. Pontiac with 1-4BBL; bhp—325 @ 4800; torque—428 lb-ft @ 3200 rpm/dual-exhaust system/3-speed stick with Hurst shifter/heavy-duty clutch/ heavy-duty springs, shocks, stabilizer bar/special 7.50 x 14 red-line high-speed nylon cord tires (rayon cord whitewalls optional at no extra cost)/14 x 6JK wide-rim wheels/high-capacity radiator / declutching fan / high-capacity battery (66 plate, 61 amp. hr.)/chromed air cleaner, rocker covers, oil filler cap/bucket seats/standard axle ratio 3.23:1 (3.08, 3.36*, 3.55* to 1 available on special order at no extra cost). **And some of our extra-cost Performance Options:** engine: 389-cu. in. Pontiac with 3-2BBL (Code #809); bhp—348 @ 4900;

torque—428 lb-ft @ 3600; 3.55:1 axle ratio standard with this engine option/4-speed with Hurst shifter (gear ratios 2.56:1, 1.91:1, 1.48:1, 1.00:1, and 2.64:1 reverse)/2-speed automatic with 2.20:1 torque converter/Safe-T-Track limited-slip differential (Code #701)/3.90:1 axle ratio available on special order with metallic brake linings, heavy-duty radiator and Safe-T-Track/handling kit—20:1 quick steering and extra-firm-control heavy-duty shocks (Code #612)/high-performance full transistor (breakerless) ignition (Code #671)/tachometer (Code #452)/custom sports steering wheel (Code #524)/exhaust splitters (Dealer installed)/wire wheel discs (Dealer installed)/ custom wheel discs, with spinner and brake cooling holes (Code #521)/console (Code #601).

Available only with heavy-duty options at slight additional charge.

the GTO makers—Pontiac

PONTIAC MOTOR DIVISION • GENERAL MOTORS CORPORATION

limited-production cars. The FIA (Federation Internationale Automobile) actually owned the name. They were using it to define a special racing class. In Italian, the term meant "Gran Turismo Omologato," or, translated to English, "Grand Touring Homologated." The Ferrari and the Pontiac were both indeed Grand Touring Cars. Both cars had been homologated (assembled from parts produced by the same manufacturer for different products into one end-product). In the

case of the Pontiac GTO, it was very simple. We took the 389-cubic-inch engine that had been designed and built for the full-size car and stuffed it into our new, lighter-weight intermediate Tempest/LeMans.

The same applied to Ferrari. They had a sophisticated dual overhead cam V-8 engine they had been

Though the two-door post had a more rigid body than the two-door hardtop and also provided a better seal against the elements, the two-door hardtop looked cooler, and style was as much a part of muscle-car mystique as outright performance.

Several years ago at GTO's Association of Americas annual convention in Denver, my colleague Dave Anderson and I got to share many, many hours of conversation with Russ Gee and Bill Collins about our favorite subject—the GTO. To a youngster like Dave, the stories seemed almost implausible. To me, they reinforced the great memories of the era we lived through at Pontiac.

One of General Motor's greatest strengths had been the division rivalry—you know, the Chevy versus Pontiac versus Oldsmobile thing. Although the divisions did share many components (sheet metal, frames, and such), it was the drivetrain, ultimate styling, and packaging that created the unique personalities of each division. Each division had private engineering garages at the Milford Proving Grounds, where they fiercely protected their innovations to the end. The development of the GTO was one of those closely and fiercely guarded secrets! After Gee and Collins had assembled the prototype, DeLorean took it for a test drive at the Proving Grounds. Upon his return, DeLorean instructed Gee to park the car in the corner of Pontiac's garage, cover it up, and not breath a word about it— under the threat of losing his job!

Gee did as instructed. However, knowing just how much fun driving the yet-to-be-named GTO was, he couldn't resist. As Gee recalled to Anderson and me, "It was an early Saturday morning when I decided to take the car for a drive on the grounds. I saw no other employees, so I felt secure in bringing the car out. As I accelerated, grabbing one gear after another, I looked down track only to see a senior Oldsmobile engineer standing along the wall. I said to myself, 'This is it! You are going to get fired!' I brought the car to a stop. He commented on how well the car seemed to perform and inquired if it was anything special. I told him we were testing a new camshaft design and he seemed to buy it. I put the car away, back under cover, and never brought it out again."

Others have caught on.
But they haven't caught up.

Imagine, for a moment, that you are in charge of designing an answer to the GTO. And that this has been your task since The Great One first rumbled into reality, sending shock waves through your offices.

Each year you've sent your answer into the streets. And, each year, seen it change into something merely mediocre alongside GTO's Hurst shifter, bulging hood scoops and Wide-Track. And, this year, humiliated by an incredible new kind of bumper.

And just when you're getting the hang of its extra-cost Ram Air (yours will surely out-GTO GTO next year).

you find Pontiac has improved theirs. With a new high-lift cam, larger swirled exhaust valves, new freer breathing combustion chambers.

When the Car of the Year is improved even before the year is over, can your car ever catch up?

The Great One by Pontiac

Answers for 6 color pictures, specs and decals of the Great Wide-Tracks? Don't be. Send 35¢ (50¢ outside U.S.A.) to: '68 Wide-Tracks, P.O. Box 888, 196 Wide-Track Blvd., Pontiac, Michigan 48056

using for racing. They decided to install it in a street version of their race car. They called it a GTO, and it, too, was a homologation. Ferrari, however, was using the name incorrectly, as by FIA standards, a manufacturer had to build at least 100 vehicles to qualify for use of the name. Ferrari never came close. As the name GTO was property of the FIA, neither Pontiac nor Ferrari could copyright it, nor could either one prevent the other from using it.

Building and naming the car was one thing. Getting it approved for production by General Motors was quite another, and it was a job that DeLorean dreaded. As the story goes, DeLorean had shown the car to general manager Pete Estes and sales manager Frank Bridge, explaining how timely it would be to kick off the 1964 model year Tempest/LeMans with

The GTO predated Ford's groundbreaking Mustang, which introduced to the American market the European long-hood, short-deck proportions that would soon come to define the muscle car.

the GTO. Bridge, an old GM soldier and not a car guy, didn't exactly jump up and down at the idea.

An even bigger and more difficult hurdle was an internal policy stating very clearly that no GM car could be built with more than 10 pounds of total vehicle weight per cubic inch of engine displacement. You didn't need to be a rocket scientist to figure out that this car, weighing in at about 3,500 pounds and powered by a 389-cubic-inch engine, would not meet that rule.

There was no way that the Engineering Policy Committee, the corporate group that policed the divisions, would ever approve a 389 Tempest as a model. It would have been foolish even to submit it. It was time for some creative thinking to find a way to move this car forward.

We learned that the committee only had interest in "new" models and did not get involved with approving options. Bingo! Why not offer the 389 engine simply as an option, only available on the top-of-the-line LeMans Coupe and Convertible models? That way, it wouldn't need corporate approval.

Thus, the GTO was born!

Before styled wheels were available, hubcaps with fake knockoff spinners were about as cool as it got.

All rise for

Now Sell It!

One day, I was called into a meeting arranged by Pete Estes, along with John DeLorean and Frank Bridge. When first shown the GTO, Bridge made it perfectly clear that he did not need it. "Frankly," he stated, "this thing is going to be a real pain in the ass." Bridge was a good sales manager. Along with moving cars, he was also responsible for dealer relations. A good factory sales manager would nearly always take his dealers' side whenever possible. Just as he had done before when Knudsen pushed for more performance imaging, Bridge, in the case of the GTO, did not believe that the dealers needed a "teenage hot rod" in their showroom. Pontiac was doing fine, the 1963 full-size car had been one of the most successful we ever had, and the division was maintaining its solid third place in sales, behind only Chevrolet and Ford. Bridge was not a marketer, and he did not understand image and the impact on the entire line this exciting new Tempest GTO could have.

I sat in the corner watching DeLorean patiently deal with Bridge. Estes was silent, almost like a referee. DeLorean was passionate; after all, this was his car. He was also aware of corporate politics, and he wanted Bridge to commit to five thousand units so the car could be pre-sold to the dealers before the corporation ever found out it existed. The more Bridge protested, the angrier DeLorean became. Estes, who had a talent for handling these kinds of issues, finally turned to Bridge and said, "Come on, Frank, you know you and your guys can sell five thousand of anything."

Estes had hit Bridge right in the middle of his ego.

With a forced smile, Bridge responded, "All right, I'll put out a memo, and we'll turn it over to the Zones. We'll let the district managers go out and see what kind of action they can drum up. If they

In the days before air conditioning was common on cars, convertibles were much more popular. It was only natural that Pontiac would offer a convertible version of its new GTO.

24

By giving the hot new Pontiac the same alpha-numeric destination as Europe's most prestigious sports car, John Z. DeLorean sent a message to the world that Pontiac was serious about performance.

can take five thousand orders, I'll commit to it. But I don't want any more, and I bet you'll have trouble selling those first five grand."

Of course, we all know now that Bridge's prediction turned out to be a joke. Sight unseen, the dealers placed orders for the five thousand cars in a matter of days. This is just what Estes and DeLorean needed to sell the GTO to GM management. The first five thousand cars were literally gone in a few weeks, with most dealers ordering replacements right away. Armed with over 15,000 new dealer orders, both Estes and DeLorean knew that the corporation would not want to make Pontiac management look irresponsible in front of their dealers by cancelling the car.

That made it easy for the corporation to approve the project, not only for Pontiac, but for Chevrolet, Oldsmobile, and Buick too! After all, those extra cars had not been planned. This could be the start of something big.

Though the GTO was DeLorean's car, a great deal of credit has to go to Pete Estes, who put his GM career on the line. This all took place on his watch as general manager of Pontiac. Had management taken a hard line and stuck to their rule, or had the GTO been an initial sales flop, it could have resulted in a black mark on Estes' record. That did not happen; all the same, Pete Estes is largely responsible for the existence of the Pontiac GTO.

As its status was questionable and the final approval of the GTO was belated, it was intentionally omitted from Pontiac's 1964 full-line catalog. After Pontiac began shipping GTOs to dealers, we threw together an exclusive catalog featuring one of the most outstanding headlines of all time, written by Roger Proulx, one of the ad agency's best copyrighters. The line "GTO: A Device For Shrinking Time and Distance" captured the car marvelously. The catalog talked about the special GTO option and its specific features and specs, carefully not overselling performance, which was purposely understated.

Although the corporation had blessed the initial order, we were worried that somebody at GM might change their mind and pull the plug. We did not over-promote speed. In fact, we were not totally confident in how the public was going to react to the car. With its late approval, we had not scheduled any prime-time television commercials or regular newspaper or magazine advertising. The only advertising we ran for 1964 was black-and-white insertions in *Auto Enthusiast* magazine. These black-and-white ads have become Pontiac classics, with headlines like, "I wouldn't stand in the middle of the page . . . That's a Pontiac GTO coming at you." Even I was uncertain whether the car was going to survive, so I ordered a backup for my personal driver. It was a white, four-speed, 421 HO Catalina Hardtop Coupe. Needless to say, it never got built once we knew for sure there was going to be a GTO. My first GTO was a four-speed Grenadier Red Sport Coupe with Tri-Power.

The machined-aluminum dash contributed to the GTO's European aesthetic.

The optional fake-wood steering wheel had to be large to provide enough leverage to turn the front wheels, given that power steering was an option.

Modest sales of the GTO began in October as availability was still limited. It was not until well into November and December that any serious numbers were produced. The public's initial reaction to the car was good, and those dealers who had already been successful in selling Pontiac performance cars jumped right on the GTO. The average dealer, however, was a little slow, even a bit reluctant to get behind the car—until customers starting coming in asking about it. The Convertible and Sport Coupe models were in full production, and the Hardtop Coupe was about to come online. Additionally, the 348-horsepower Tri-Power engine option had been released.

GTO sales really came alive when the March 1964 issue of *Car and Driver* magazine appeared. The controversial cover story featured a performance comparison between the world's two most famous GTOs: the new upstart from Pontiac against the world-class Ferrari, featuring the incredible headline, "Tempest GTO: 0-to-100 in 11.8 sec."

Car and Driver Story

In what was to become perhaps the best promotion we ever put together, I leveraged a relationship with *Car and Driver* editor David E. Davis in late 1963, convincing Davis to feature a comparison test of Pontiac's new GTO against Ferrari's GTO. *Car and Driver* had just recently changed its name from *Sports Cars Illustrated* as part of an effort to reinvent the magazine, featuring more emphasis on American cars. As it turned out, even I didn't realize how timely an idea I had proposed, not only for Pontiac but also for the magazine itself.

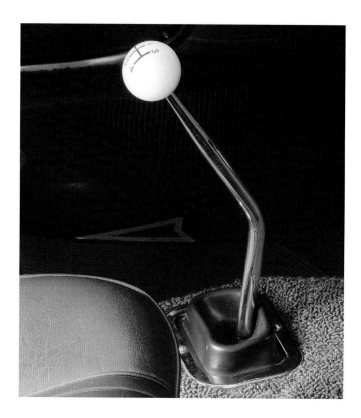

Slick-shifting Hurst linkage shifted the large cogs in the optional four-speed gearbox with buttery-smooth precision, at least when compared with the sloppy stock shifters found in other General Motors products of the era.

If you think Wide-Tracking is just a slogan, you've never been behind the wheel of The Great One.

Slogans don't straighten curves. Or conquer hills with the ease of an Alpine tram. But then, not many cars do, either. Which is why our GTO is so reverently referred to as The Great One.

The GTO's ability in the aforementioned situations can be traced partly to its standard 400-cubic-inch, 4-barrel V-8. A 3-speed with Hurst shifter. And Fastrak, redline tires that adhere to the road like glue clings to your fingers.

Great American sports also dig Le Mans, Firebird, Catalina, Bonneville and Grand Prix.

However, The Great One didn't merit *Motor Trend* magazine's "Car of the Year" accolade merely for its driving prowess. Its polished sheet metal is molded into the shape of tomorrow. And up front, the world's most fantastic bumper. So fantastic, you have to kick it to believe it.

So when you next read that Wide-Tracking in a GTO is great, don't shrug and turn the page. See your Pontiac dealer. Where test drives speak louder than words.

Pontiac Motor Division.

Wide-Track 1968 Pontiacs

The faux vents atop the hood didn't improve breathing or cooling, but they looked badass.

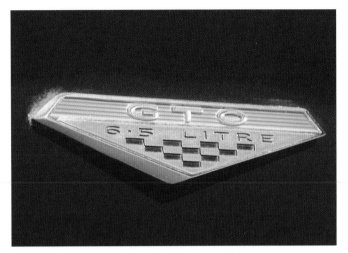

To emphasize the Euro aspirations of its new GTO, Pontiac measured the engine in cubic liters (even using the European spelling, *litre*) instead of in the American cubic inches.

I called Davis in early December 1963 to tell him about this great new car, which we were calling GTO. I explained that we knew the name was not copyrighted and that Ferrari was using it too. On the basis of the name overlap, I suggested that this could make for an interesting comparison test. As it turned out, they were looking for a way to make a statement of their own about the new direction of the magazine. This idea went a long way in demonstrating their commitment to American performance iron.

We scheduled the test to take place between Christmas and New Years, 1963. *Car and Driver* rented the Daytona International Speedway and wanted a car as early as possible. They wanted to live with it for a week or so in New York City and then drive it down to Florida. They said they would arrange to get the Ferrari.

Regardless of the testing outcome, this was going to be a win-win situation for Pontiac. Just sitting on the same track with a Ferrari, being tested by a respected magazine would certainly make an impression. For Ferrari, on the other hand, it was degrading and even ludicrous to be compared to a "lousy" Pontiac. As it turned out, Ferrari was smart enough

GTO is built for driving. So are the available buckets. They're firm. Contoured. Comfortable.

Pontiac's Radial Tuned Suspension. Worth ordering. FR78-14 steel-belted radials. Front and rear bars. Firmer shocks. Computer-selected springs.

A new shaker hood scoops cold, dense air. For more performance.

Pontiac's new 350 4-bbl. V-8 is standard. It won't disappoint you.

With GTO, you stir from the floor. 3 speeds standard. 4 available.

The Wide-Track people have a way with cars.

PONTIAC | GM
Pontiac Motor Division

Announcing Pontiac's new GTO. This tough little compact didn't just inherit its great name. It earned it.

To make its sporty new car stand out, Pontiac festooned the car with GTO ornamentation on every available surface. It worked; onlookers knew that this was a special car from any angle.

never to furnish a car. Fortunately, the *Car and Driver* guys had previously tested one.

I made the arrangements for the two Pontiac GTOs. The first one was a Nocturne Blue Sport Coupe, a "pilot car" (a pre-production model with no ID number, meaning the car could never be sold to the public) with the 348-horsepower, 389-cubic-inch Tri-Power engine, M20 wide-ratio four-speed, and 3.55:1 limited slip rear end. This was the ride-and-handling car. I special-ordered the second car, which was now a real production-line car. It was a Grenadier Red Sport Coupe equipped with Tri-Power, a wide-ratio four-speed, and a 3.55:1 rear end. The car was ordered with "sound deadener delete," a common practice to reduce weight in purpose-built factory-assembled race cars in those days. The GTO was then turned over to Royal Pontiac, the factory's backdoor performance dealer. The driveline was changed to include a close-ratio four-speed and a limited-slip 3.90 rear

end. Since the car was to be used for acceleration testing, Royal's Bobcat package was also installed. I shared with the *Car and Driver* editors the entire spec sheet detailing all the Bobcat modifications.

When it came time for *Car and Driver* to pick up the cars in Detroit, they only sent one driver. They took the blue car, and I agreed to drive the red car to Daytona, arriving the day after Christmas.

I set out on the 22nd of December in the red car with Bud Conrad, a young mechanic from Royal Pontiac who was to maintain the GTOs during the testing. We met Dave Davis, his wife, and *Car and Driver*'s managing editor, John Jerome, at the Daytona Speedway the morning of December 26. We had barely exchanged our greetings when talk started about how impressed they were and what a great car our blue GTO had been. They talked about how much fun they had with it in New York City and what a wonderful road car it was on the drive down to Florida.

I asked the *Car and Driver* team, "When is the Ferrari coming?"

They told me, "Tomorrow, we hope. There was some trouble getting the car released." I think they assumed I was smart enough to put two and two together. The next day came and went, and with it, no Ferrari. I quit asking!

Once Davis got into the red car, he would not get out of it. We spent the better part of the day making stop watch–timed runs. Quarter mile, 0 to 60 mph, 0 to 70 mph, 0 to 90 mph, and on up to well over 100 mph, over and over again. When they came up with a 0 to 60 mph time of 4.6 seconds, and 0 to 100 mph in 11.8 seconds, I knew it was time for me to shut up and watch. Our red GTO couldn't have run 0 to 100 mph in 11.8 seconds if it had been dropped right off the top of the Empire State Building.

When the March 1964 issue of *Car and Driver* hit the newsstands, the magazine's editorial literally ignited GTO sales! The *Car and Driver* cover depicted a painting of the Pontiac GTO and the Ferrari GTO tangling on a road course. The painting was, of course, a necessity, as Ferrari smartly refused to allow their car to participate in this knife fight. The spectacular cover line: "Tempest GTO: 0-to-100 in 11.8 sec" introduced not only a new kind of magazine but also a new kind of car. Pontiac had created, and *Car and Driver* had discovered, the American muscle car.

One last and important note about this significant 1964 GTO. While writing *Glory Days: When Horsepower and Passion Ruled Detroit*, I revealed the real story of the red car. Over the years, rumors had surfaced about the actual engine in that car. I had to confess that I had secretly installed a 421-cubic-inch HO engine, a close-ratio four-speed, and a 3.90:1 rear end prior to the Royal Bobcat tune-up. Many years later, in 2010, Davis and I had quite the chuckle as he expressed his consternation over having had one put over on him. This is the stuff that legends are made of. . . . After all, it was only a 421!

GOAT

Arguably, the Pontiac GTO has been credited with being the first true American muscle car. Supporters of the exciting 1949 Olds 88 with its new OHV Rocket V-8 engine will protest, as will those who believe the 1955 Chrysler 300, with its fabulous Hemi engine, started it all. Then we can't forget those folks who swear the racy 1962 Chevrolet 409 Bel Air Coupe started it all.

While these great cars did make significant contributions to the history of American performance, there really is only one GTO. In fact, there were almost a million of them built over eleven model years, and that ought to be proof enough.

The one thing that still remains a mystery, however, is that name. What does GTO really mean? I've been telling everybody about that Italian term "Gran Turismo Omlogato" and have been trying to explain the word *homologated* for over forty years. I'm still not sure everybody understands. In fact, I'm not sure even I understand.

So, why not just call it a "GOAT"? It's so much easier.

The GTO might have been aimed at the emerging baby-boomer market, but its handsome, well-proportioned, understated styling appealed to everyone.

2

Birth of the Pony Car

Randy Leffingwell

Detroit muscle cars gave enthusiasts hot rods with warranties. They also proved to be good business for the automakers. They intercepted the profits that independent speed shops earned and shifted them onto corporate spreadsheets.

Pony cars proved to be even better business because they made muscle cars acceptable, turning them into vehicles their owners could drive to work through the week, to the market on Saturday morning, and to the drag strip or the movies on Saturday night. Pony cars were the kind of muscle cars that doctors, bankers, and teachers could drive to church on Sunday morning.

For decades, historians have credited product planners and marketing types with inventing muscle cars. The common premise is that American GIs

By 1965, when the Mustang entered its second model year, there wasn't a person in the United States who didn't recognize the iconic racing-pony emblem.

About the only thing the 1962 Mustang I show car donated to the production Mustang was the name.

returned from the wars in Europe and Korea with combat pay in their pockets and a desire for speed and horsepower in their souls. But that theory doesn't go far enough, and it doesn't dig back long enough or reach out broadly enough.

During World War II, automotive engineers spent their time designing better bombsites, improved tank turrets, stronger truck suspensions, and superior

aircraft engines. Those who worked with engines and carburetion became familiar with lighter metals, higher engine speeds, and superior intake and exhaust management. They were antsy to put that knowledge into the next automobile engine they designed. Automobile engine designers invented the muscle that went into the car.

Product planners, advertising wizards, and corporate chairmen certainly had imagination and vision. They are the ones who asked for an automobile with a long hood and short rear deck, with two front bucket seats and two occasional ones in back, with red-stripe tires and four-speed floor shifts, and they chose evocative names like Mustang, Camaro, and Barracuda. They "invented" pony cars. But very few of them imagined they should ask for a 221-cubic-inch V-8 with thin walls or a 351 or a 429. Or to add two additional bolts to each crankshaft bearing cap. Or to increase the carburetor size from one barrel to two or four and to specify 780 cubic feet per minute of air-induction capacity. Mounted on a high-rise manifold. With ram air induction. In many cases, engine displacements resulted from size rules in racing classes. Engineers thrived on the challenge of dividing up the cylinder dimensions of bore and stroke.

The short rear deck of the 1964 1/2 Mustang would forever after define the look of performance.

The Mustang was an obvious choice for a car to pace the 1964 Indianapolis 500. The pace car's white-with-blue-stripes livery would soon be put to good use by a certain chicken farmer from Texas.

Eventually product planners learned to request bigger engines, often with 1 or 2 cubic inches more displacement than their competitors in order to gain bragging rights and advertising claims.

From the start of the automobile it was the engine guys who said, "Hey, we can do this to that engine. It'll make more power. Come up with something to put it in." Participation in racing validated their experiments, or else it sent them back to their slide rules. Successes led customers into dealerships to get cars with engines like the ones that won Indy or Daytona or Le Mans.

Some enthusiasts have accused Ford Motor Company of sitting out the muscle-car era. Perspective is important here. So is a bit of historical background. Following a tragic racing accident in Europe in June 1955, the American Automobile Manufacturing Association (AMA) spent a couple of

While the point of the Mustang was to appeal to youthful buyers, Ford didn't turn away those who were youthful at heart. Many Mustang buyers just wanted sporty looks and were content with the base six-cylinder engine.

years fussing and finessing language in reaction to the crash. Then it issued a statement recommending that its members—Ford, Chrysler, General Motors, Packard, Hudson, Studebaker, Nash, Willys, Crosley, and the rest—refrain from participating in motor sports or from using any kind of speed events or even performance language to promote and sell their products. Dutifully all the manufacturers signed on. Better, they reckoned, that they police their own behavior before Washington's legislators did it for them.

The recommendation affected the auto industry much the way the Eighteenth Constitutional Amendment in 1919 that prohibited the sale of alcohol impacted liquor manufacture and consumption. Automakers still went racing, but did so by going out of their backdoors instead of through the front lobby. Engineers enjoyed vacation time working the pits during major events. Plymouth, Dodge, Pontiac, and Chevrolet managers became particularly adept at

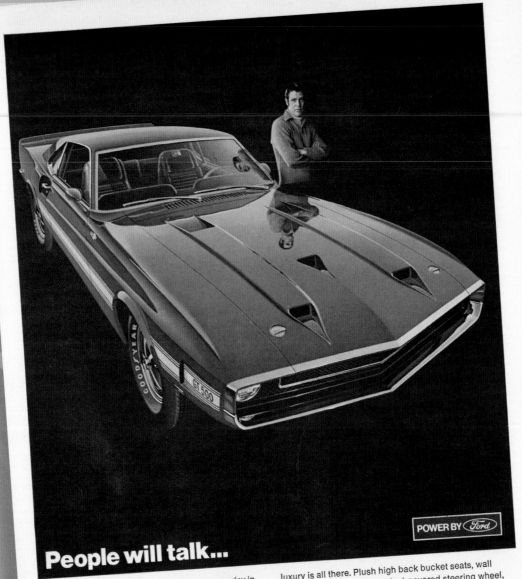

People will talk...

You better believe they'll talk if you show up one day in a Shelby GT. After all, this is a car with a reputation. And the wherewithal to back it up. Your choice of 351 or 428 Ram-Air V-8 heads the list, followed swiftly by front disc brakes, built in roll bar, air-ducts for brake cooling, a suspension that's the toughest set-up this side of Daytona, and your choice of a 4-speed manual or 3-speed automatic transmission . . . even 5 racy "Grabber" exterior colors . . . the whole shot. In short, the sort of thing people want in a car that looks that mean.

But, somehow you don't expect to find *luxury* with this kind of performance machine. But with Shelby the luxury is all there. Plush high back bucket seats, wall to wall carpeting, padded vinyl-covered steering wheel, tasteful touches of simulated teakwood trim, door mounted courtesy lights, bright trimmed pedal pads and sequential turn signals. True elegance and luxury!

So go ahead! Open the doors, invite the folks in and really give them something to talk about.

Shelby GT for 1969

Shelby GT 350/500
SHELBY COBRA

67

camouflaging factory support by claiming they could not control their customers activities.

Ford Motor Company obeyed the AMA recommendation, and not just because Henry Ford II, a conservative man, believed he marched upon a higher moral plane than the others. "The Deuce," as Ford II was known, also revered his Ford Division vice president and General Manager, Robert S. McNamara. This seemingly dispassionate number cruncher saw no value in competing against other carmakers except in parts prices, sales numbers, manufacturing efficiencies, and profit margins. Numbers inspired McNamara and they motivated him.

Lieutenant Colonel McNamara arrived at Ford just after World War II, part of a group of recently released U.S. Air Force officers who had applied a system of statistical analysis to keep track of aircraft, the missions they flew, and their spare parts and munitions. Known as the Whiz Kids, this group quickly became the Quiz Kids. They asked countless questions of everyone in every department as they forced order onto Ford's post-wartime chaos. Some of them left after accomplishing their mission; others stayed and rose through the corporation's ranks.

McNamara's calculating practicality acknowledged that utilitarian transportation had a purpose. Others climbing through the company hierarchies wondered if there might be more to the business than that. McNamara's contribution to Ford's balance sheet and history was the functional Falcon. It sold 417,174 units in its first year, impressive numbers for a new product. But Lido Iacocca, a mechanical engineer with a flair for marketing and sales, suspected the car might have sold even better if it had looked more exciting.

Ford introduced the Falcon on October 3, 1959, one day after Chevrolet debuted its unorthodox rear-engine, air-cooled Corvair, and about three weeks before Chrysler's Valiant first appeared. (Chrysler registered the name Falcon for its Valiant but it entered the application 20 minutes later than Ford at the AMA office, thereby losing the rights.) Within a month, Ford Falcon sales soared, eclipsing and then humbling its competition. The car earned the nickname, "King of the Compacts." The Deuce promoted McNamara to corporate president.

The most potent Mustang offered in the early years was the GT equipped with the K-code version of the 289 V-8.

Chevrolet planners may have overhead Iacocca. Or the Corvair's quirkiness might have inspired them as they watched their sales figures settle at half what Ford had achieved with the Falcon. Repositioning theirs as a specialty car, Chevrolet introduced a sportier Monza model in April 1960, offering bucket seats and a floor-mounted four-speed shift. GM promoted it as a "poor man's Porsche." This analogy helped generate 144,000 sales.

Eight months later, right after the November elections, the nation's new president John Kennedy asked McNamara to join his cabinet as his Secretary of Defense. McNamara transferred to Washington D.C. in December. Within Ford Motor Company, the Falcon lost its champion. Lee Iacocca, impatient in the wings, stepped onto the stage. The board of directors named him Ford division general manager as McNamara left.

For years Iacocca kept notebooks that he filled with ideas. He already had formed an afterhours think tank he named the Fairlane Committee after the hotel in which the group met to plan Ford's

future. He invited division product planning manager Don Frey to join, along with his special assistant Hal Sperlich. Another five decision makers filled out the table. They surreptitiously updated the Falcon, though it took Ford until the following April to confront the Corvair Monza challenge with their new Falcon Futura. Then Iacocca convinced the Deuce to exile McNamara's next idea to European sales only. This car, called the Cardinal, was an even more cerebral compact car than the Falcon, with a V-4 engine and front-wheel drive. It didn't fit anywhere in Lee's notebooks. The committee launched themes, first "The Lively Ones," and next came "Total Performance." The Fairlane Committee made another appeal to Henry Ford II, pointing out GM's and Chrysler's flagrant and headline-grabbing racing participation, inducing him to abandon his commitment to the AMA performance and competition ban.

The Fairlane Committee returned the Blue Oval to stock car racing and launched it in drag racing.

The K-code engine cranked out 271 horsepower thanks to a solid-lifter camshaft, 600 cfm Holley carburetor, and hotter ignition.

Then it partnered with Englishman Colin Chapman to provide engines to fit behind the driver's seat in Chapman's Lotus cars to enter the Indianapolis 500.

Marketing surveys told Iacocca that Ford customers missed the two-seat Thunderbird but Lee's notebooks interpreted that as a longing for sportiness more than limited passenger capacity. The Fairlane Committee also monitored sales of the Corvair Monza.

"That's how it all started," Don Frey recalled in an interview in September 2005, "watching Monzas. We started watching Corvair registrations. The car was a dog so Chevy planners put in bucket seats and gave it a new name and it started to sell. We all recognized there was something going on there." The Falcon Futura remedied the individual seats and floor shift details, but the car still ran Ford's

Ford turned to Carroll Shelby to provide the hottest version of the original Mustang, the Shelby GT350.

101-horsepower inline six. It needed more power to enhance its image, and engineers had it coming. They bored out the "Thin Wall" 221-cubic-inch V-8 engine to displace 260 cubic inches, and they installed that in the new Futura Sprint. It represented a turning point, an identity change not just for the car but also for the company. Prior to the spring launch, Henry Ford II toed the line behind Robert McNamara and

Ford heralded his corporation as a safety company, not a performance automaker. When Iacocca presented McNamara-like numbers that quantified Falcon sales lost to the sportier Monza, Henry changed his tune, embracing the next theme: "Total Performance: Powered by Ford."

Ford won Indianapolis. It claimed stock car series titles and drag race championships. Iacocca was energized, and he challenged Frey and Sperlich to create a new "special Falcon," one true to Lee's

The first Mustang to pace the Indianapolis 500 was painted white with blue racing stripes; Carroll Shelby's Mustang earned those stripes. The original 1965 Shelby GT350 was really a race car for the streets.

In 1966, the Mustang still had the market niche it had created all to itself. For Ford, the Mustang was like printing money.

belief that McNamara's Falcon would have sold even better if it had a "particular look."

Iacocca had fallen in love with the long hood/ short rear deck configuration back in 1946. "I got crazy about [it] based on the original Continental Mark I," he admitted to Richard Johnson in an interview for Johnson's book *Six Men Who Built the Modern Auto Industry*. A Ford recruiter whom Lee met while studying at Lehigh University drove one. Iacocca became addicted to its shapes. "I had a book called the *Auto Universum*, which had all the cars. I looked at all the cars that had those proportions and I said, 'Wow. If we could get that particular look they'd think they'd died and went to heaven.'"

He had the authority to demand it. He ordered Gene Bordinat, head of Ford Styling, to adopt the long hood and short deck and "make it look like a two-seater, but for four passengers—with enough room in back so it's not a joke."

His idea came with no guarantee, however. Henry Ford II always had final authority, and he made everyone work for approval. While the corporation had achieved great success with the Thunderbird in 1955 and with the Falcon, the Edsel humbled them in 1958. The Futura Sprint was not exactly sprinting out dealer doors either. Don Frey campaigned hard to sell this new car.

Ford's partnership with Shelby to build high-performance Mustangs paid huge dividends at the racetrack. Shelby GT350s dominated road racing, and a handful of drag-racing variants like the one shown here set records across the country.

You'd love to answer the call of Mustang? Good! There are three new ways: hardtop, fastback and convertible! Standard features include bucket seats, carpeting, floor-mounted shift, Ford Motor Company Lifeguard-Design safety features. And there are options galore, like

Stereo-Sonic Tape System, SelectShift automatic transmission that also works manually, V-8's up to 390-cu.-in., power front disc brakes, bench seat, tilt-away steering wheel, AM-FM radio, air conditioning. Smitten? Great! May we pronounce you "Man and Mustang?"

'67 MUSTANG
Bred first...to be first

"Each time I proposed it," Frey recalled, "Mr. Ford said no. Then, finally, the afternoon after the fifth meeting, we were in the design studio looking at some new proposals. Mr. Ford walked up behind me and whispered in my ear—I'm going to use, exactly, the same language he did—'Frey,' he said, 'I'm tired of your fucking car. I'm going to approve it this afternoon, and it's your ass if it doesn't sell.'" It hardly was an endorsement. Iacocca took over the sales job from there.

"Once we got the styling going," he explained to Johnson, "I used to take Henry over to the studio. I made sure I got him involved and he put his imprint on the car in a hurry. He got in the back and said, 'Well, shit, I thought this was a four passenger [car] but there's not enough room for me. Add an inch or two.'"

The first-generation Mustang, as marketing soon named it, essentially was a reconfigured and re-skinned Falcon. Gene Bordinat's stylists reversed the proportions of the short nose/long tail compact and, on the same chassis, created Iacocca's dream car. Design and engineering hurried it into production

The Hurst car-rental company even got in on the Shelby craze, commissioning Shelby to build a special variant for its rental fleet.

in 18 months, half the normal gestation for a Ford product, and it met its planned nationwide introduction date: Friday, April 17, 1964. Ad agency J. Walter Thompson booked exclusive television commercial airtime during a 30-minute slot the night before, filling ABC, CBS, and NBC airwaves and giving some 29 million viewers, according to A.C. Nielsen's ratings, several opportunities to see the car during prime time shows. The next morning and over the weekend, 2,600 newspapers ran stories and published paid advertisements.

On its first day, Ford dealers sold 22,000 Mustangs. By New Year's Eve 1964, the total reached 263,434, and by the close of business April 17, 1965, Iacocca's sporty four-seater had sold 418,812 cars in its first year. Iacocca had beaten McNamara by 1,638 cars. Marketing characterized the staid, economical Falcon as a compact, in company with the Valiant, by

Shelby celebrated the 1967 makeover of the Mustang by mounting an extra pair of headlights in the center of the grille. This got the small automaker in trouble with various departments of transportation, and the lights were moved out to the edges of the grille early in the production run.

then a Plymouth product. Chrysler moved forward with a redesign, but its symmetrical shapes front to rear failed to capture many imaginations and their new cab-forward fastback Barracuda defied the long-hood-short-deck proportional ideals with the largest back glass in any automobile up to that time. Studying Mustang sales figures, Chevrolet upgraded their Corvair with a turbocharger, devising a more potent Corsa model, and they reviewed the Chevy II that they

With competition in the form of the Chevrolet Camaro, Ford upped its Mustang game for 1968, introducing special editions such as the California special.

developed to compete with the Falcon. They headed back to work.

The Mustang created its own genre, an entire new category that, for lack of a better term, became known as the "pony car." For Ford, it only got better from here.

The Deuce and his accountants had committed $40 million to develop the Mustang. This was generous considering he allocated $36 million for McNamara's all-new Cardinal. However, because so many pieces came from the Falcon, the huge development and "fixed costs" normally associated with a new model weren't there. What's more, everyone floated cautious sales projections despite an appealing $2,321 base price for the coupe.

"They based the financial planning money on 75,000 units a year," Iacocca explained to Richard Johnson, "so they didn't carry the fixed cost load the way they accounted for it. So all of a sudden

Ford also offered a High Country Special, which featured a higher state of tune for regions with high elevation, such as Colorado.

[with] no fixed costs we sold 500,000 the first year. They couldn't count the money fast enough. . . . The fixed costs were all paid for. The Falcon paid for it all."

Faced with unexpected success and such vast profits, product planners and engineers suggested variations. Marketing wanted a "super deluxe interior," Bob Negstad explained, "with leather and built-in air-conditioning in the dash, not a hang on. And we wanted to do higher series wheels and tires."

Negstad was one of the chassis engineers who developed the coupe and convertible Mustangs. He also had worked on the two-door, two-seat, mid-engine roadster that engineering devised in 1962 as a prototype known as Mustang I to fire up consumer interest in Ford's coming products. While it excelled in that task, it represented a direction neither Iacocca nor Henry Ford II wanted to take, so development went no further. Once the four-seater was in production, Negstad and his colleagues, eager to instill some of the two-seater's sporting character, pushed for rear disc brakes and an independent rear suspension.

Bordinat's stylists created a fastback concept that they revealed to Iacocca in May 1964. He approved it immediately and fastback production commenced at the Dearborn River Rouge plant and the new facility at San Jose, California, on August 1, as a 1965 model. Magazine reviewers who already adored the coupe and convertible fell in love again with the new fastback. While no independent rear suspension arrived underneath the car, its angled back window added enough weight over the rear axle to improve handling.

Total Performance: Powered by Ford included the pony car. However, Don Frey had no luck getting Sports Car Club of America (SCCA) president

One of the things that made the California Special special was a different rear-end treatment, lifted off the 1967 Shelby models (which in turn borrowed a rear-end treatment from the Mercury Cougar).

John Bishop even to consider the Mustang. Frey had invited a racer/entrepreneur named Carroll Shelby into Ford World Headquarters back in early 1962 to consider his request for a handful of Ford V-8s that he intended to install in a British sports car plus some cash to do the work. Chevrolet recently had turned him down. Shelby had won the 24 Hours of Le Mans in 1959 driving an Aston Martin. His value to Ford Motor Company soared, however, when Frey learned that although Carroll had raced privately owned Ferraris in America, he loathed Enzo Ferrari, a feeling he shared with Henry Ford II. Between Corvette and the Italian carmaker, Carroll had his sights set on two racing targets that the Deuce intended to vanquish.

For both Shelby and the Deuce, the loathing of the Italian auto magnate was personal. Shelby's hatred of Enzo Ferrari stemmed from Ferrari expecting the

Texan to drive one of the Italian's racecars *gratis*, believing that an American hillbilly like Shelby should be honored just to have a seat in one of the magnificent machines bearing the crest of the prancing horse.

The Deuce's hatred of the man likewise stemmed from a perceived personal slight. Ford Motor Company had tried to acquire Ferrari in 1962 after Enzo dangled a carrot at the end of a long line. Don Frey, an Italian speaker, managed negotiations for months. Prices and sales conditions varied with lunar phases until Ferrari abruptly ended everything. It had been a ruse to force fellow Italian carmaker FIAT to act. Ford recalled Frey and his team and ordered them to build a Ford racer that would "kick Ferrari's ass."

Shelby got his engines and the Shelby A.C. Cobra was born. Cobras won the SCCA manufacturers championship in their first year, while in England a small

To compete with the upstart Camaro, which featured a big-block engine option, Ford offered the 390-powered Cobra Jet midyear in 1968.

crew worked night and day to develop the Deuce's sleek low racer called the Ford GT40, referring to its roof height. Ford Advanced Vehicles ran the initial competition efforts. Frey eventually invited Shelby in to advise and then manage the GT40 racing program as well.

For the Mustang, Shelby learned from SCCA's John Bishop that Ford's pony racer had to be a two-seater with either a modified suspension or a modified engine. Shelby could yank out back seats and install a roll bar. The Texan decided that an upgraded suspension would be more effective than upgrading the already powerful V-8 engine, so he decided

The hot ticket for the Cobra Jet was to get the Super Cobra Jet package, which got you all sorts of good bits aimed at making the Mustang a terror in the quarter mile.

to focus on installing improved suspension pieces. His Cobra-creating engineers set to work making the Mustang competition ready. Shelby and his Cobra-creators joked about what to name it. They estimated the distance from one of their buildings to another at 350 feet.

"Then call it the GT350," Shelby explained in an interview in 2005. "If the little car's a winner, it won't matter. And if the sonofabitch is no good, then it won't matter either." Bishop's staff approved the cars and Mustangs went racing in SCCA B Production.

It was becoming a thing with Carroll: His Shelby GT350 Mustangs followed his Cobras to victory, claiming ownership of the grids and the corners and the checkered flags at SCCA events through 1965. They won five of six SCCA regional divisions and the national championship.

Shelby still offered the small-block GT350 in 1968, but most buyers of high-dollar Mustangs wanted the big-block GT500.

Everyone wanted to get in on the "Mustang Mania" buying frenzy. Hertz Rent-A-Car operated a sports car club, renting Corvettes to qualified customers from a couple dozen airport and city locations around America. Shelby's friend Peyton Cramer researched Hertz history and discovered that their original business in Chicago rented cars painted in a distinctive black-and-gold color scheme. He scheduled a meeting with Hertz executives and marketing teams and he had a GT350 painted black with gold stripes. It scored another Shelby win: For 1966, Hertz bought 1,003 of the cars, requesting that Shelby add an "H" to the designation. Hertz occasionally was inconsistent with its paperwork. Most of the cars reached rental outlets in black and gold, but nearly 200 arrived in other color combinations. The first 85

came with four-speed manual gearboxes, but then Hertz insisted on automatics. For drivers older than 25, Hertz rented the GT-350H for $17 per day and 17¢ per mile.

Regular production Mustangs for 1966 ran a new base 200-cubic-inch inline six offering 120 horsepower, and three variations of the 289-cubic-inch V-8 that delivered 200, 225, or 271 horsepower. Shelby's (and Hertz's) GT350s delivered 306 horsepower while some cars appeared with Paxton superchargers as a one-year-only option, pushing output to 390 horsepower. Ford redesigned the body for 1967, widening and lengthening it slightly. A 390-cubic-inch-displacement V-8 arrived on option lists, producing 320 horsepower. Shelby's new

The top-dog Mustang in 1968 was the Shelby GT500KR.

While the original 1965 Shelby GT350 did not come as a convertible, by 1968 buyers could get any Shelby topless, even the mighty GT500KR.

"B" pillar along the fastback. These resembled the markers racers used to identify their cars to pit crews and timing personnel during night races. However, these fixtures projected red lights forward and to the side, a capability granted only to emergency vehicles. Shelby had to spread the center headlights and remove the glowing red markers. The recall embarrassed Ford Motor Company.

Chevrolet's "pony car," the Camaro, reached dealers as a 1967 model. Ford had enjoyed more than two full model years to establish benchmarks in enthusiasts' minds. Camaros mimicked the Mustang's long nose/short tail appearance, but Chevrolet offered only coupe and convertible bodies. Plymouth gave its Barracuda fastback a new look with revised front and rear ends.

428-engined GT500 models for 1967 provided buyers with 355 horsepower.

Following a few vehicle statute problems with Shelby's 1967 GT350 and GT500 models, Ford reclaimed GT assembly from Shelby's shops in California, moving the assembly back to Michigan for 1968, where the division kept tighter control on design, options, and quality. This model year marked a kind of tipping point in the configuration and popularity of the Shelby models. In the GT350's first year, Carroll assembled a production race car for the streets, a commodity that buyers insisted they wanted until they owned one. Then they complained that it was too loud and it rode too roughly. Suspension modifications for 1966 reduced noise, vibration, and harshness, and sales increased. Still, some potential buyers whined that a distinctive high-performance Mustang should look more distinctive. For 1967, two of those distinguishing appearance features included front bright headlights mounted together in the center of the grille and red lamps installed high on the

By 1969, Ford offered so many Mustang variations that a car like this convertible GT could get lost in the crowd.

The car initially appeared only as a coupe and a proportionally improved fastback. Later in the model year their convertible arrived.

For 1968, the American Society of Automotive Engineers (SAE) revised the method in which it quoted engine horsepower from gross figures to net ratings. As a result, power outputs registered lower than the year before. Ford introduced its 302-cubic-inch-displacement V-8, destined to replace the base 195-horsepower 289 by year end. The 302 delivered 230 net horsepower with four-barrel carburetion. The 390 remained in the lineup providing 280 net horsepower but still developing 325 net for the GT model. The big news was bigger displacement and greater horsepower as Ford offered a 390-net-horsepower "High Performance" 427-cubic-inch engine and a conservatively rated 428 "Cobra Jet" (CJ) engine derived from the Police Interceptor powerplant that produced 335 net horsepower. The 1968 Shelby GT350 carried over the

The upscale Mustang customer could select the formal Grandé version.

tuned 289 with 306 horsepower while the GT500 utilized the 335 horsepower 428 CJ package.

For 1969, Ford widened and lengthened the Mustang again, offering buyers a notchback coupe, fastback, and convertible once more. A new Grandé trim package for the notchback gave Dearborn planners the upgraded interior and exterior materials they first had proposed in early 1965. Performance packages appeared with GT, Mach 1, Boss 302, and Boss 429 designations that indicated trim features as well as engine variations. Options under the hood ranged

from a 200-cubic-inch-displacement 115-net-horsepower inline six through versions of the 302 delivering 220 net horsepower with a two-barrel carburetor and 290 net in the Boss 302 with a four-barrel. A new 351-cubic-inch V-8 came next, offering 250 net horsepower through a two-barrel carburetor or 290 net with a four-barrel carburetor. The Q-code 428 Cobra Jet in the GT500 gave buyers 335 net, the R-code 428 "Super Cobra Jet" with "Ram-Air induction," essentially a factory-delivered drag racing engine, rated a

1969 Trans-Am Boss 302 Mustang

Nearest thing to a Trans-Am Mustang that you can bolt a license plate onto.
Boss 302

Our objective was to build a reasonably quick machine with a tight power to weight ratio. Power starts with a lightweight, precision-cast short-stroke 302 C.I.D. block. Top it with 10.5:1 heads with inclined 2.23" intake and 1.71" exhaust valves under aluminum rocker covers. Bolt on an aluminum high-riser manifold and a 780 CFM 4-barrel Holley carb. Add low-restriction headers and large-diameter dual exhausts. Fire it with dual-point ignition. You get 290 hp at 6000 easy revs. And it can be tuned for more.

Power gets to the road via a high-capacity 10.4" clutch and a trigger-quick 4-speed box. There's a "Daytona" axle with a standard 3.50 ratio. You can order it with a 3.50, 3.91 or 4.30 locker axle if you're that kind of guy. Wheels are styled-steel 7" rims with F60 x 15 fiber-glass belted tires. (These smokers are 2 inches wider than F70's. We had to flair the wheel wells a bit to get them on.) Quick-ratio steering, floating-caliper front disc power brakes, competition-

handling springs, shocks, front stabilizer bar and front spoiler are standard. Comes with a collapsible spare tire in case you're wondering about trunk space. One body only—'69 Mustang SportsRoof. Options include rear spoiler, backlight louvers, power steering and chrome plated (15 x 7) styled steel wheels.

Objective accomplished. You're invited to inspect one at your Ford Dealer's Performance Corner. Also on display at various Trans-Am events coming up soon.

For your free copy of Ford's 1969 Performance Buyer's Digest, write: Performance Digest, Department HR, P. O. Box 1000, Dearborn, Michigan 48121.

MUSTANG Ford

The Boss 302 version was Ford's tool for the then popular Trans-Am racing series, designed to compete with Chevrolet's Z/28.

deceptive and very conservative 360 net horsepower, while Ford's powerhouse Z-code Boss 429 delivered 375 net horsepower.

Performance offerings for 1970 changed subtly as the division deleted the 390 from Mustang option sheets. Ford suspended production of Shelby GT350 and GT500 models in mid-1969 as demand waned.

Dealers sold off remaining 1969 models through 1970; state motor vehicle departments required 1970 registrations so Shelby Mustangs assembled in 1969 received new vehicle identification number (VIN) tags. Production 302 models ran with 220 net horsepower while the Cleveland-built 351 yielded 250 net horsepower with a two-barrel or 300 net with four-barrel carburetion. Outputs for the Q- and R-code 428s and Z-code Boss 429 remained unchanged from 1969.

Another new (and larger) body appeared in 1971. Ford offered this Mustang only as a sleek fastback or a convertible. The base 250-cubic-inch-displacement inline six yielded 145 net horsepower and the 302 V-8 developed 210 net. The 351 Cleveland-built engine output ranged from 240 net horsepower with a two-barrel carburetor through 285 net as the four-barrel

The Boss 429 was really just a vessel in which to homologate the new 429 NASCAR racing engine.

Cobra Jet, and it peaked at 330 net in the Boss 351 configuration. The Boss 429 entered its last year of production delivering 370 net horsepower.

For the Mustang and the glory of Ford's pony car, the best days were passing. Auto insurance company lobbyists had gained the ear of Washington legislators. Insurance premiums punished sporty youngsters who bought sporty cars, charging annual fees equal to half or more of the purchase price of the car if manufacturers rated engine output above a certain level. Ford's base inline six delivered 98 net horsepower for 1972, while its most powerful Q-code High Output 351 Cleveland, using a single four-barrel carburetor, produced just 266 net horsepower.

Ford was not alone in adjusting to political change. Camaros had introduced and, by 1970, had withdrawn 427-cubic-inch-displacement V-8s in cast iron and even in aluminum that produced 425 net and even 460 net horsepower. For 1970, output peaked

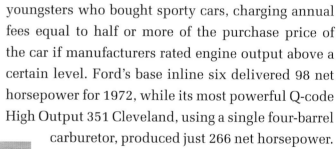

The 1969–1970 Shelby Mustangs were the last of the original breed. By that time, Ford had taken production of the cars in-house, and Shelby involvement was minimal. These final cars were little more than just another option package.

Plymouth and Dodge, each with handsome new coupe and convertible bodies for their Barracudas and Challengers, forced similar horsepower withdrawal on their customers. The legendary hemispherical-head V-8 engines offered buyers 425 reliable net horsepower until the 1971 model year. Chrysler divisions delivered their last half-dozen hemi engines by mid-1971, and the corporation discontinued its 440s that offered buyers as much as 390 net horsepower through three two-barrel carburetors. For 1972, Barracudas and Challengers offered only 110-net-horsepower, 225-cubic-

at 375 net horsepower for customers who bought an SS-optioned Camaro with the 396-cubic-inch big-block. Model year 1972 saw output figures retreat to 255 net from Chevrolet's 396 while its inline-six base engine matched Ford's with 100 net horsepower.

The Boss 302, which was an exceptionally handling, well-balanced performance car, remained popular in 1970.

inch-displacement inline sixes, 150-net-horsepower, 318-cubic-inch V-8s, or optional 340-cubic-inch engines delivering 240 net horsepower.

As if those power reductions were not enough to hobble the pony-car genre, convertibles disappeared too. Carmakers feared that open cars were next on Washington's enemies list. Manufacturers grew gun-shy following the publicity that consumer activist Ralph Nader earned accusing Chevrolet's Corvair of being "Unsafe at Any Speed," (the title of his book and his safety campaign). No automaker wanted to appear under the congressional magnifying glass. Voters were losing their sons in a war fought in Southeast Asia, one calculated and

The shake hood scoop was optional for 1970 Boss 302 buyers.

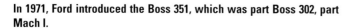

In 1971, Ford introduced the Boss 351, which was part Boss 302, part Mach I.

The Boss 351 came at a time when performance was on the way out, but it was still a strong performer and one of the quickest cars on the market at the time.

promoted by Secretary of Defense Robert McNamara. After those kinds of tragedies, it seemed unthinkable that young people also might die in crashes caused by overpowered automobiles. The American Automobile Manufacturer's Association felt no need to issue another recommendation. American Motors, Chrysler, Ford, and General Motors, the four remaining carmakers, took the responsibility on themselves. Racing skulked around to the back doors again. Auto executives looked out, released a deep breath, and believed they had avoided a mugging that had their name on it.

Then in mid-1973, the Organization of Petroleum Exporting Countries (OPEC) notified the world that it intended to punish Israel's allies for their loyalty by reducing production by 5 percent each month until Israel withdrew from occupied territories. The United States already imported more than 25 percent of the crude oil it needed each year. This threat was significant. Gasoline prices at the pumps began to climb, recasting those Clevelands and Cobra Jets as costly legacies of recent hedonism.

On October 17, OPEC instituted what it called "oil diplomacy." It cut off any nation from purchasing oil it had available if that government had supported Israel in its conflicts with Egypt, Syria, and Jordan.

This particularly meant the United States. Other announcements followed that inflated the price of a barrel of crude oil. It settled—temporarily—at $11.65, nearly four times the price it commanded the previous December (about $59 today, adjusting for inflation). Gasoline at the pump jumped from 38 cents per gallon to 84 cents (the equivalent of $4.08 per gallon today, adjusted for inflation) between October 1973 and March 1974. Pony cars with their 6- and 7-mile-per-gallon consumption no longer inspired plans for cruise nights. Auto executives Lee Iacocca and Henry Ford recalled that a shareholder several years earlier had asked why cars always had to grow in size. "Why can you just leave a sports car small?" she'd asked.

Anna Muccioli, the stockowner, had given Ford and Iacocca something to think about. Newspapers reported that during that annual meeting in March 1968, Henry Ford II answered her and the audience, explaining that his company tried "to build the kind of car that we will sell most of to the general public, so that is our basic approach." That approach—to car design and world politics—meant the end of the original incarnation of the pony car, and of the muscle car in general.

The Mustang soldiered on throughout the grim 1970s and 1980s, but the Boss 351 was the last of the original high-performance Mustangs. A couple of generations of Mustang buyers would come and go before the car was once again a true muscle car.

When they were Just Cars

Rare times made for rare cars during the golden age of muscle cars

Joe Oldham

There was actually a time in America when you could walk into any Chrysler-Plymouth dealer in the country—there were several thousand of them—and purchase as many Hemi Barracuda convertibles as you wanted. There were no limits. There were no shortages. Hemi-powered Barracuda convertibles were not in short supply. For two full years, from September 1969 to August 1971, had you wanted to buy 20,000 of them, Chrysler Corp. would gladly have built and sold them to you.

But in those two model years (1970–1971) that Hemi-powered Barracuda convertibles were offered, only 25 were built—14 in the 1970 model year and 11 in 1971. Of those, two 1970 units were built for Chrysler itself to serve as press demonstrators and were eventually sold as used cars. So only 12 Hemi 'Cuda convertibles were actually bought by paying customers in 1970, and 11 in 1971.

Today, a Hemi 'Cuda convertible is one of the most valuable American cars built in the post–World War II era. When Joe Oldham tested a new one, it was just a not-very-good car with a leaky transmission.

Why?

Judging by the frenzy these cars cause on the ultra-rare occasion when one shows up at a car show or auction, you'd think they were highly desirable cars and Chrysler should have sold a ton of them. So why only 25 in two years?

I'll tell you why—they were lousy cars, and nobody wanted them back then. How do I know? During the golden era of muscle cars, I worked as a writer for Magnum-Royal Publications in New York City, publisher of auto magazines such as *Hi-Performance Cars*, *Speed and Supercar*, and others. It was my job to track test, street race, and photograph all the muscle cars of the '60s and early '70s. I lived through the muscle-car era, not as a consumer or collector, but as an industry insider with every conceivable hot car at my disposal.

Back then, I looked at the cars I had to write about as, well, just cars, not coveted, collectible *objets d'art* that would someday sell at auctions for

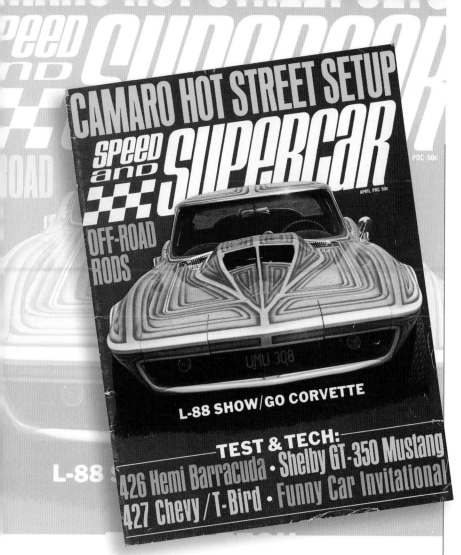

Back in the golden era of muscle cars, Joe Oldham had perhaps the coolest job around—testing the beasts for car magazines.

hundreds of thousands, or even millions, of dollars. They were just cars. Just as you can pick up a copy of any car magazine today—or log on to any automotive website—and find a review of a new Hyundai Sonata, back then you could find the same sort of information about muscle cars, and it was my job to drive and review the new cars of the day—Hemi Barracuda convertibles, Ram Air GTOs, W30 Olds 442s, and Cobra Jet Mustangs.

They were just cars.

And I'm telling you, 14 Hemi Barracuda convertibles were all Chrysler *could* sell in 1970. And they could sell only 11 in '71.

I can also tell you this without equivocation: Chrysler muscle cars were

There are college dorm rooms that have less square footage than a Hemi air cleaner.

terrible to drive as everyday vehicles. I used to dread it when my boss, Marty Schorr, assigned me to pick up some Mopars and do a story on them. Yes, I actually dreaded having to drive Mopar muscle cars, especially Hemi-powered cars.

Granted, the 440-powered Wedge cars ran very well. They had excellent low-end torque and could hold their own on the street with anything out of GM—Pontiac GTOs, Oldsmobile 442s, Buick Gran Sports, Chevy Chevelles, and Camaro SS-396s. (Ford was a nonentity on the street until the 428CJ engine came along in 1968.) But as cars, the Mopars were crudely built compared with GM or Ford, with cheap plastic upholstery, knobs falling off, windows that didn't seal properly, carpeting that didn't lay flat, etc.

The Hemi? Dodge Chargers, Coronet R/Ts, Super Bees, Plymouth GTXs, Road Runners, and other Mopar models with the Hemi engine were even worse. They compounded poor fit and finish with an engine that would barely run on the street and weighed 200 pounds more than the wedge. That's right. The Hemi engine, as it came from the factory in showroom stock condition, would barely run on the street.

HEMI HEAD

MOPAR
DO NOT WASH OR OIL
NORMAL OPERATION — CLEAN HOUSING CLEAN FILTER

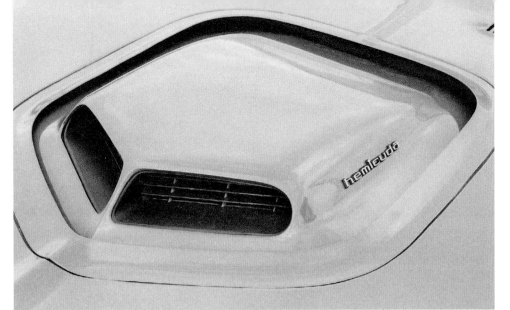

Having a Hemi under the hood might be impressive in the parking lot, but in stock form, it was less impressive out on the road.

Hey, it wasn't the engine's fault. Let's face it. It was a race engine, introduced in 1964 to do one thing—win races in NASCAR and NHRA competition. Did you ever look at a Hemi cylinder head? The ports are the size of a Los Angeles sewer. The valves look like New York City manhole covers. And it has two huge four-barrel carbs sitting on top of it. The engine was designed to run at full throttle on a track at 6,800 rpm. As such, it developed zero low-end torque.

Then in 1968, things got worse with the addition of the first federally mandated emission controls—retarded ignition, leaned-out carburetion, and air pumps. When you punched the throttle on the street, the Hemi coughed, sputtered, and choked. Literally. That's why we always had to have a team of Mopar tuning experts, headed by Al Kirschenbaum, high-performance manager of the Rockville Centre Dodge dealership, accompany us on every Mopar track test.

Performance on the street was pathetic, and we said so in print many times. So did a few other magazines. We ran several Hemi versus Wedge comparison tests back then, and the Wedge car always won—until the tuners stepped in and got the Hemi going. Even Hemi fanatics had to give ground on the engine's showroom stock performance. We actually received death threats at the office if we didn't "lay off the negative Mopar stories." They even called my mother names. Of course today, 42 years later, all these cars have been over-restored, and all the Hemi's faults have been sorted out and corrected, and they all run like they just came out of Richard Petty's engine shop.

The four-speed cars were a total joke. The Chrysler A833 four-speed transmission would hardly shift. You had to muscle it hard to get it from gear to gear, and the factory floor shifter would ram your right hand into the dash on every 2-3 shift. The later much-revered pistol grip shifter was only slightly better. No wonder everyone ordered the three-speed TorqueFlite automatic.

With all the negative press, it's no wonder hardly anyone ordered a Hemi-powered or four-speed car—unless they were going to race it on a track. Street rats stuck with the 440 Wedge-automatic combo and rightly so. The Hemi option was $800 extra, plus

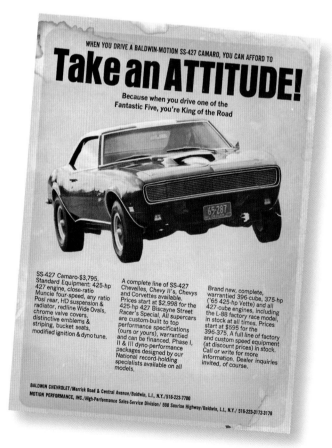

Rare? Check. Valuable? Yep. Sexy? You bet. Just one problem—it wasn't a very good car.

$200 more for the four-speed, but the 440 ran better out of the box. Why would you want a Hemi four-speed? Hardly anyone did.

The sales figures tell the story with crystal clarity. If Chrysler had orders for 50,000 Dodge Hemi-powered Superbees in 1968 rather than the 166 it actually built, don't you think it would have built them? I assure you, Chrysler would have—gladly. The same holds true for all the other weirdo Mopar engine-body combinations you now see at auctions selling for gazillions.

Hey, I'm not just picking on Chrysler here, although it's easy to pick on them because the 426 Hemi was so ubiquitous and was available in so many different body styles. Rare Mopars abound. They only built 60 of those and only 104 of these and so forth. In total, though, Chrysler built thousands of Hemi-powered cars throughout the 1960s.

Ford's 1969–1970 Boss 429 Mustang is another perfect example of a dumb, but beautiful, car that resulted from stuffing a race engine in a street body. Ford took a huge engine with gigantic ports and valves that it knew wouldn't run on the street, then put a mild cam in it and stuck a tiny 735-cfm four-barrel on top in an attempt to make it streetable. Topped off with federally mandated emission controls, Ford executives wondered why we blasted the car in the press. Never mind that

Ford needed to put 500 cars on the street with the 429 engine to meet NASCAR's homologation requirements. While the Boss 429 didn't beat many competitors in stock form, it did beat that number; Ford built 858 Boss 429 Mustangs in 1969.

The 1969 ZL-1 Camaro was another car that was built only to qualify for the NHRA's Super Stock C and D classes, but the NHRA classified it as a factory experimental car, the F/X class, which by that time had morphed into the funny car class, and ZL-1s were running against all-out drag-racing cars, making the engine instantly obsolete.

it would hardly run on the street and it was slow. Yes, *slow*. It felt like you were driving not a 429 Mustang but a 289 Mustang—that is, until you got the thing up over 4,000 rpm. Mercifully, Ford built only 859 of them in '69 and 501 in '70.

The fact is, all the car companies built small numbers of certain engine-body combinations to compete in specific sanctioned race events. In 1963, Pontiac built only 14 Super Duty 421 aluminum-front-end "Swiss cheese" Catalinas, and Chevy just 50 aluminum-front-end, aluminum-engine 427 Z-11 Impalas. In 1969, Chevy built only 69 ZL-1 aluminum-engine Camaros. Ford built just 199 solid-lifter 429 Super Cobra Jet Torino Cobras in '71. But these manufacturers acknowledged that they were building specialty limited-production race cars—street legal, yes—meant to be raced on a track and just enough of them to allow them to qualify as "regular production" models under the rules of the race sanctioning organizations. For instance, there was no attempt by Chevrolet to pass off a Z-11 427 Impala convertible model for street use.

Each all-aluminum 427-cubic-inch ZL-1 engine took 16 hours to assemble by hand, which was a large part of the reason the engine was a $4,000-plus option (on a car with a base sticker price of $2,621.00).

These manufacturers had to build a certain number to meet the rules, but no one said customers had to buy them. There are plenty of stories, for instance, of COPO 9560 ZL-1 1969 Camaros sitting on dealers' lots well into the 1970 model year because no one wanted a $6,000 Camaro with an aluminum 427 engine that would barely run. Don't you wish you had one now?

Not every muscle car buyer necessarily wanted the highest output engine available. Many buyers didn't need or want it because there were viable alternatives. Pontiac 389-400 Firebirds and GTOs are perfect examples of this. The standard four-barrel 400 or 400 HO provided strong street performance without the extra five hundred bucks for the Ram Air IV. For another thing, although rare in their own right, Ram Air IV-powered cars ran fine on the street without all the finicky drama of a 426 Hemi. So did a W30, a Stage 1, an LS6, a 428 Cobra Jet, a 440 Six-Pack Mopar, and, for that matter, most of the other available high-output engines of that era.

One of the reasons most people didn't drop the extra dough on special packages like Pontiac's Ram Air IV was that the basic cars such as this Pontiac Firebird 400 were fast enough for many.

Some of these combos were rare because of high option cost, availability, or other reasons, not because they were lousy cars to drive. And some of the rarest cars are rare simply because the manufacturer started building them late in the model year and only had time to build a small number before the model year ended.

What all this "limited-production" stuff did was produce some ultra-rare cars. Happily, I got to drive many of them back in the day. At the time, I didn't know they were rare. In fact, I couldn't have cared less. I had no idea I was driving some of the rarest muscle cars ever produced. When I drove these cars back then, I was just doing a job, and they were just cars, not revered rarities valued higher by collector fanatics than Fabergé eggs.

I was just lucky—lucky enough to have lived through that era, lucky enough to have the job I had, and lucky enough to still be earning a buck telling tales of the muscle car. I just wish I had bought all 14 of those '70 Barracuda ragtops.

1970 Plymouth Hemi Barracuda Convertible (One of 14)

Encounter one. This car, which turned out to be so historic and so iconic, was a pain in my ass from the first time I laid eyes on it.

It was sitting in a corner of Chrysler's press fleet garage on East 43rd Street in New York City with a pool of red liquid oozing out from under the car.

Chrysler's unibody muscle cars lacked chassis rigidity even in coupe form; lop off the top to make a convertible, and the car became a rolling spring. It looked damned good, though.

455 OLDS • 426 'CUDA TESTS

HI-PERFORMANCE

CARS

MAY PDC   50c

427 CAMARO Blown Fuel Setups

Dyno-Tuning The Ram-Air GTO • Funny Car Roundup
Chrysler 300 '55-'65 History Plus Hemi Road Test

If Joe had had a crystal ball when he tested the Hemi 'Cuda convertible for the May 1970 issue
of *Hi-Performance Cars* magazine, he would have bought it on the spot, sat on it for 35 years,
then sold it at the peak of the Hemi market, netting a $1,000,000 profit.

Two days before, Marty Schorr, editorial director of Magnum-Royal Publications and my boss,
had given me instructions: Moon Mullins, then–
East Coast public relations manager of Chrysler
Corporation, had left a 1970 Barracuda convertible
in the press fleet garage for us. It had the new-for-'70
hydraulic-lifter 426 Street Hemi engine. Go pick up
the car, photograph it, run it at the track, go street racing, generally live with it for a week, then write it up.

I borrowed a flashlight from the garage attendant
and looked under the car. There was a visible drip
coming off the transmission. I wondered if I would
make it home to Queens, much less all the way to
Raceway Park in Englishtown, New Jersey, the following day. It did but with the transmission slipping
badly all the way.

The next morning, there was yet another pool of
transmission fluid under the car. I checked the trans
dipstick, and it was at least two quarts low. I filled it
up with gas and transmission fluid at the local service
station and made my way to Raceway Park, where Al
Kirschenbaum met me. Al had performed the factory
prep on this car at his dealership, Rockville Centre
Dodge, where he was the high-performance manager.
I had asked him to assist me at the track on this test.

Al told me a little about the car as I shot some
still photos. This was the first '70 Hemi Barracuda

convertible built and delivered with black body
side moldings. Chrysler's PR department didn't
want the moldings on the car, so they had been
removed at Rockville Centre Dodge's body shop.
What's more, despite being built as a Barracuda
convertible, the car did not have some of the
cosmetic trim pieces that all other '70 'Cudas
carried, such as the hockey stick decals on the
rear fenders. There were simply none available
at the factory on September 27, 1969, the day
this car was built.

He did not think the "slight" trans fluid
leak would be a problem.

I asked Al to jump in the car and pull to the
line for a run. He did so, brake revved the engine,
and promptly blew off the transmission cooler
line, dumping fluid all over the starting line at
Raceway Park.

74

With a little tweaking, Oldham was able to get the Hemi 'Cuda convertible to run a 14.30-second quarter mile, which was about par for the course for a Hemi of the era, but slower than a well-tuned 340 'Cuda, which cost $800 less than the Hemi.

plugs. The best timeslip was a 14.30 at 97 mph, accompanied by lots of wheelspin and tire smoke and zero traction. This was usual stuff for box-stock Hemis in those days. Several weeks later, Kirschenbaum informed me that his guys had recurved the distributor, rejetted the carburetors, installed new colder plugs, and generally supertuned the car. Back at Raceway Park, it had turned a 13.80 at 103 mph.

My notes also indicate that the Hemi 'Cuda was the perhaps best handling Mopar I had driven to that time and that the fit, finish, interior materials were above average for a Mopar. So despite the trials and tribulations the car had given me, I had been favorably impressed overall.

After adding yet another quart of trans fluid, I returned the car to the press fleet garage. Subsequently, another editor from Magnum-Royal picked up the car and wrote it up for another of our magazines. My report appeared in *Speed and Supercar* magazine.

I never saw the car again, nor did I even think about it. I went on to work for the Hearst Corporation and eventually became editor-in-chief of *Popular Mechanics*. In the meantime, this particular car became a cult object and one of the most coveted cars in the car collecting world.

As I said, it was the first Hemi 'Cuda convertible built in the 1970 model year. It was one of only 14 1970 Hemi 'Cuda convertibles built overall, and one of only 9 built with an automatic transmission. It was the only red-on-red Hemi 'Cuda convertible built and was used as the model for the Danbury Mint's Hemi 'Cuda convertible die-cast replica

Encounter Two. In 1989, 19 years after my article was published, I was walking through a car show in New Jersey with old pal Cliff Gromer, the editor

After calming down track owners Rich and Vince Napp, I called a flatbed and had the car hauled back to the press fleet garage in New York City. Test over for now.

About a week later, I received word that the car was repaired and ready to go at the garage. Upon arriving at the garage, the first thing I did was crawl under the car and take a look. Damn, there was still a transmission leak, but nothing like it was. On the way home, the transmission still didn't feel right when it shifted, and the trans selector linkage was loose. It was hard to tell what gear the trans was in.

The next day, back at Raceway Park, we ran the car mercilessly. We made a couple dozen full-throttle runs down the strip, did at least a dozen burnouts for photos, and ran the tires off the car on the handling loop.

My notes from that day tell me that the car ran pretty well for a stock Street Hemi despite having tired

While the flexible convertible chassis wound up like Chrysler's infamous torsion-bar suspension in corners, the car didn't handle that badly by the standards of the day.

of *Mopar Action* magazine. We saw a red Barracuda convertible down the row of cars. I thought it looked familiar. As we got closer, I said to Gromer that it looked like the car I had tested in November 1969. But there was one way to tell for sure; I looked under. Yes, there it was—the transmission leak forming a small pool of red oil under the car! It was the same car!

Wayne Hartye, a Mopar collector from New Jersey, was the owner then and even had my article framed up as part of his car show display. He promptly agreed to let Gromer do an article on the car for *Mopar Action*. It appeared in the April 1994 issue. Hartye told us he thought the car was worth maybe $150,000 at that time. We were amazed at how the car had appreciated in value. Again, I lost track of it.

Encounter Three. In 2006, Gromer received a call from the then-owner, Bill Wiemann of Fargo,

North Dakota, who had acquired the car and was in the process of having it restored by the great Roger Gibson of Roger Gibson Restorations in Scott City, Missouri. And would Joe Oldham like to drive it when it was completed?

So 35 years later, I had yet another encounter with this same car. And there it was, sitting in Bill Wiemann's private Mopar museum in the Arizona desert. I couldn't resist. I had to look under. The transmission leak had finally, mercifully, been repaired.

When I opened the driver's door and looked at that red interior, it was definitely weird. The interior was still all original. So when I sat down in that seat, my butt was in exactly the same place it was 35 years before. I felt very much in touch with the past, almost like I was going back in time.

The next day, I drove myself back to the future with Wiemann and Roger Gibson, who had flown in for the day. We dropped the Hemi 'Cuda's top and were off to Speedworld Raceway Park in Surprise, Arizona. I climbed into the driver's seat and settled in. The seating position was better than I remembered, but the steering column still felt too long and too close. All that was forgotten as I twisted the key and the big 426 Street Hemi bellowed to life.

Man, what a sound. No amount of modern technology can match the sheer thrill of being the master of 426 cubic inches of leashed fury. I sat there with the twin exhaust pipes gurgling, just grinning.

We headed out to the track, and the ride was stiff, but that's how all Hemi cars were. The steering was a little loose and overboosted, but that's how all Mopars were.

Then I mashed my foot down through the linkage detents, and all eight barrels opened up. Delicious! We heard that delicious sound several more times on the way to the track, each time backing out of it just north of a hundred. At the track, I did several full-throttle burnouts, and we ran the car through the traps just like back in the day. On the clocks, the car

ran a couple of mid-14-second passes at just under 100 mph, eventually recording a best of 14.32 seconds at 99 mph—almost identical to the box stock times of 35 years before.

And guess what? The transmission was doing it to us again, not quite shifting properly on the 2-3 shift, even hanging up on one run, and the gear selector lever felt loose. The more some things change, the more they stay the same.

At a Barrett-Jackson auction in Scottsdale several years ago, a '71 Hemi 'Cuda convertible sold for an even $2 million. So what might this one be worth? Some Mopar hobby observers tell me that this particular Hemi 'Cuda convertible may well be worth as much as $4 million.

Like I said, shoulda-woulda-coulda bought all 14 of 'em.

In stock form, the Hemi might not have been a drag-racing terror, but it had more than enough power to overwhelm the skinny bias-ply tires of the day.

1969 SS-427 Baldwin-Motion Camaro (One of One?)

Baldwin-Motion? Think of that organization as the Yenko-Nickey-Dana-Berger of the New York City area. The cars rolling out of Detroit at the time were pussies compared with rolling stock carrying the Baldwin-Motion badge. Baldwin Chevrolet in Baldwin, New York, teamed with Motion Performance, also in Baldwin, to produce what could arguably be called the ultimate muscle cars of the sixties.

Starting in 1968, you could buy a Baldwin-Motion 427 Camaro, Nova, or Chevelle, even though the largest factory-available engine was a 396. And if you ordered the Phase III package on any of these

Although used to advertise Baldwin-Motion's Phase III package, Oldham knows for a fact that this car was in a more mild state of tune. He knows this because Baldwin-Motion used his personal car in the photo.

Although the 427-cubic-inch engine was a stock L72, that was not a bad thing since the L72 cranked out 425 horsepower.

cars, the 425 factory horsepower was only a starting point that soon faded away as huge three-barrel carburetors and L-88 cams were added.

For Camaros, Chevelles, and Novas, the base car for all SS-427s was the hottest combination you could get from the Chevy factory at the time—the L78 396 engine, rated at 375 horsepower. Everything started with the scrapping of the 396 and the substitution of an L72 427 rated at 425 horsepower in stock form. From there, you could add 38 different performance options. Backing the engine in most Baldwin-Motion cars was a close-ratio Muncie M22 four-speed, any ratio 12-bolt Positraction rear axle, a heavy-duty suspension and radiator, fat tires, chrome valve covers, special emblems and stripes, bucket seats, a modified ignition, and a full dyno-tune. In 1968, that package went out the door for $3,795, *even the brand-new Camaro*. I remember the take-out 396/375 engines being sold by Motion in crates for $595.

But there was more, way more. Maybe you wanted the fearsome Phase III package. Then your Camaro was *guaranteed in writing* to run 11.50 at 120

Baldwin-Motion also featured Oldham's car at its 1968 Thanksgiving hot rod show display at the New York Coliseum.

mph on the drag strip. The Phase III engine packed 500 horsepower thanks to the addition of a three-barrel 950 cfm Holley on a high-rise aluminum manifold, special solid-lifter cam with 0.580-inch lift, Mallory ignition system, clutch-type fan, and more. Even with the Phase III setup, your tab would run only $4,998.

Motion had even hotter cars they sold for race duty only, even though they were all street legal. The ultimate power trip was provided by a vehicle with a Motion-massaged and blueprinted L-88 427 under the hood.

I was lucky enough not only to drive them all at one time or another, but I actually owned one of these fantastic cars. The Baldwin-Motion SS-427 Camaro

pictured here was my car, owned by me. Although there are no production records for Baldwin-Motion cars, Motion owner Joel Rosen has told me he doesn't remember building another triple black SS-427 '69 Camaro like mine and, perhaps, only built around 20–25 Camaros for the entire 1969 model year. So my car was an extremely rare muscle car—perhaps one of 20 and maybe even one of one.

Even in the annals of Baldwin-Motion cars, this was a famous one—the black car that was used in the Motion Performance display at the 1968 Thanksgiving weekend hot rod show in the New York Coliseum and also on the famous "Wanted" poster and "Outrageous" ads for 1969 Baldwin-Motion cars. Yeah, that was my car.

It was a relatively mild combination, as it was to be my daily driver around the New York City area: stock L72 427/425 engine, Hooker headers, breakerless ignition, chambered exhaust, three-speed Turbo Hydra-Matic trans, 4.10 Posi, disc brakes, triple black (black paint, black interior, black vinyl roof), Super Sport package, VE3 body-colored front bumper, no spoilers, no SS stripes, hood scoop, hood tach, add-on Sun gauges, 15x8 Keystone Kustomag wheels, G70-15 front and L70-15 rear Mickey Thompson tires, and SS-427 emblems everywhere.

All you had to do was keep peeling off the hundreds, and Rosen would build it any way you wanted. The sticker price was just over $6,000, but I got a "professional discount," actually paying $5,100.65 for the car.

After almost completing the car to my specifications, Rosen asked if I would mind if they used my car in advertising and showed it at the holiday hot rod and custom show at the New York Coliseum. No problem. When the car was photographed for the ads, it still had the SS stripes on the side and was fitted with American Racing Torq-Thrust wheels and blackwalls. By the time it was shown, the decal hockey-stick stripes had been removed, and it had been fitted with different wheels. Other than that, it was as I had ordered it.

Converted to my final specs, I took delivery in late November 1968. I couldn't wait to drive it home. Response was instantaneous at any speed in any gear. Despite the huge rear tires, first gear was just a spinning, smoking fight for traction. Banging the horseshoe shifter into second at 7000 rpm produced a loud screech from the rear tires. Third was a

Oldham had Baldwin-Motion tone down the look of the car before he took possession of it. The sleeper look made it that much sweeter when he beat his opponents, which happened every single time he ever raced them.

How much did Oldham like the Baldwin-Motion Camaro? Enough to buy one with his own money.

headlong charge into three-digit speeds—or oblivion. I quickly learned to respect the tremendous potential for catastrophe while driving this car.

And this was just on the way home.

My Camaro was never beaten on the street while I owned it, and I went up against everything on wheels that winter. One night stands out in my memory. I remember making a grand tour of the New York street racing haunts—Cross Bay Boulevard, Connecting Highway, Nassau Expressway, Mitchell's on Seventh Avenue, Adventurer's, Gun Hill Road. I must have put dozens of light-to-light runs on my Camaro. I went up against anything that came along—GTOs, street rods, Mopars, Oldsmobiles, Mustangs, mid-50s Chevys. Everything and anything. My SS-427 Camaro took them all.

The best run I remember was on the Connecting against a guy with a big mouth and a Hemi-powered '68 Road Runner. He was the self-proclaimed "King

of the Connecting," and his "worked" Hemi had never been beaten by any stock-bodied car—until he met the Chevrolet big-block gods that night and the SS-427 emblem between my taillights.

What was even better than street racing in this car was just cruising. The head-turning ability of this car was incredible. Everybody looked. It was something special, even to me, jaded as I was by my unlimited access to all things automotive. It had that hairy, menacing look that said, "Hey, don't mess with me, or I'll blow your freaking doors off."

I took my SS-427 Camaro to the track only once. At Suffolk County Raceway in Westhampton, New York, on a cold December day with zero traction and the Hookers closed, it ran a best of 12.74 at 107.5 mph. I always wanted to try it with the headers open and slicks on a warmer day but never got the chance.

The car was stolen two months later.

Unfortunately for Joe, some thief also liked the Camaro and stole it not long after Joe bought it.

GRAND SLAM!

Torino wins 1968 NASCAR,
USAC and ARCA championships.

And Cobra's coming on for more!

Torino started strong by taking the first five places in the first race it entered, the 1968 Riverside 500. Torino finished strong, too. Specially modified Torinos won all three stock car racing crowns. Boss drivers Dave Pearson, A. J. Foyt and Benny Parsons did a lot of hard charging to get us there.

What's all this got to do with you and our new street machine? Plenty. Something as quick and mean as Cobra doesn't happen until you do a batch of triple-crown-winning Torinos. Cars that go fast grow slowly! With Better Ideas born in the heat and hustle of stock car racing.

Take a good look at Cobra by Ford. Standard 428 CID 4-barrel V-8 rated conservatively at 335 horses. (The *largest* standard engine in any car in its class.) Competition suspension with staggered rear shocks

GRA
Torino wins 1968 NASCAR,
USAC and ARCA championships.

And Cobra's coming on for more!

Of all the cars I've owned, this is the one I most regret not having today. Not because it might sell for hundreds of thousands at an auction but because this was the coolest car I ever owned—and maybe the coolest car I ever drove.

1968 1/2 428CJ Ford Mustang (One of 1,299)

In the spring of 1968, halfway through the model year, Ford offered a new option for Mustangs—the 428 Cobra Jet engine for $420.96 extra. Make no mistake, this engine saved Ford from being a total washout in the muscle-car sweepstakes. In '69, they followed up with the Boss 302, Boss 429, and Mach I packages, and Ford's bacon was saved. But the '68 1/2 428CJ Mustang started Ford back on the road to respectability.

When it was announced, the 428CJ sounded like another half-assed attempt by Ford to interpret the high-performance street market, and, frankly, it looked pretty weak. A smallish 735-cfm four-barrel Holley sitting atop a low-rise aluminum (later changed to cast iron) intake manifold from the old 390 Police

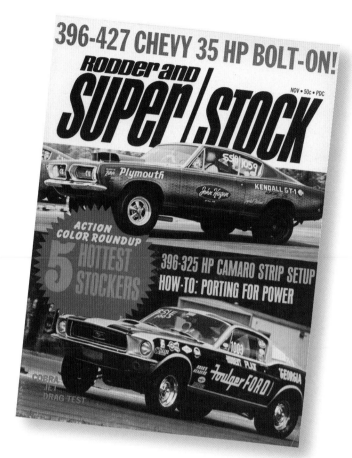

In the spring of 1968, Oldham tested something that he hadn't driven before: a competitive Ford muscle car.

Interceptor package, the old 406 cylinder heads (albeit with a 10.6 to 1 compression ratio and 2.06-inch intake and 1.625-inch exhaust valves), and a rather mild hydraulic cam with 270/290 degrees intake/exhaust duration all sitting on a standard 428 passenger car block didn't sound like much on paper.

But all these R-code CJs did come standard with a functional hood scoop and ram air setup that had a flapper on the air cleaner that opened when you pounded the accelerator pedal. Also, as part of the option package, you got a heavy-duty 80 amp battery, a 55 amp alternator, dual exhausts, an HD cooling system, chrome engine dress-up items, and cast-aluminum rocker covers.

Altogether, though, it sounded downright lame compared with other street engines around in '68— like Mopar's solid-lifter 426 Street Hemi and Chevy's solid-lifter 427 big-blocks. The 428CJs deliberately underrated 335 horsepower at 5,400 rpm and

A quick visual inspection of the R-code 428 Cobra Jet engine, with its smallish carburetor, didn't inspire much hope that the Mustang would impress at the drag strip.

At least the 428 CJ Mustang had a functional hood scoop that fed a ram air system.

440 lb-ft of torque at 3,400 rpm didn't help the engine's street cred.

Turns out, though, that Ford's engineers got it *exactly right.*

I knew Ford finally had something competitive when, on a Wednesday time trials night, we took our test car to Raceway Park in Englishtown, New Jersey, and it ran 13.59 at 105.62 mph *on the very first run.* That was before we even pumped up the tires. Later

that night, we worked the timeslips down to 13.20 seconds at 107 mph with no tuning whatsoever. This was all with the stock F70-14 Goodyear Polyglas tires and a 3.89 rear axle in our four-speed fastback GT.

High school physics formulas will tell you that you need about 450 horsepower to accelerate a 3,400-pound car to 107 mph in a quarter mile. So we all knew the power ratings given the 428CJ were laughable, but it worked well for the guys drag racing these cars. They fell into very favorable classes under NHRA rules and dominated wherever they ran. But it was on the street where they really shined. That meant torque, and lots of it.

Had someone run some accelerometer tests on a 428CJ Mustang, I'm sure they would have determined that the engine was

In stock form, the 428 CJ Cobra could turn a 13.2-second quarter mile, indicating that actual power output was considerably higher than the 335-horsepower rating Ford gave the car. With a little bit of tuning, the car was capable of much more.

actually putting out maybe 500 lb-ft of torque. How cool was that? Lots cool when some asswipe in a 396 Chevelle pulled up next to you at a light, revved the engine, and looked over at you. Lots cool when the next thing he knew, you were getting rubber in third gear and he was looking at your tailpipes.

I had several chances to do just that in the week I spent with our test car. Most dorks had no idea what the plain-Jane Mustang GT fastback was. Most thought it was some 390 Mustang with an ugly hood scoop glued on. The only run I remember losing was to a '67 427/435 tripower Corvette. One loss. Not

bad for a week of street racing. I can tell you this: after that week, Mustangs in particular—and Ford in general—were looked upon with a lot more respect around the New York City street racing haunts.

That's what it was all about in the muscle-car 60s—respect on the street. The '68 1/2 428CJ Mustang put Ford right back in the game when it looked like they were about to veer off track for good.

Ford only built this car on special order in '68 and, apparently, only 1,299 guys knew about it and were smart enough to order one. How many survive? I've never seen one yet at any car show or auction, so I assume they all met their intended fate—having

Ford's 428 CJ Cobra had the performance to match its badass looks.

their wheels run off and driven flat into the ground. In a way, that's probably the greatest respect you can give a car.

1968 426 Hemi Dodge Superbee (One of 74)

When I picked up this test car, I had no idea I was about to drive one of the rarest cars of the muscle-car era. I had no idea they would only build 166 1968 Dodge Superbees with the 426 Hemi engine (according to *Old Cars Weekly Muscle Car Field Guide*) and that, of those, only 74 would have TorqueFlite automatic transmissions behind the engines. I didn't know that, in a few minutes, I would be driving one of 74 ever produced.

Nor would I have cared. It's common today for cars like this to sell for more than a hundred thousand a pop. But then, it was just a car, and all I knew was that I was getting paid to go street racing for a week in a brand-new Hemi Superbee and somebody else was even paying for the tires.

My Superbee was a post car, painted the yellowest yellow I had ever seen. I also noticed that someone

had bolted on a set of incorrect Chrome Road Wheels (Magnum 500 style) and F70-14 tires. All Hemis came standard with 15-inch wheels and F70-15s, but obviously the PR guys wanted this press car to look its sharpest in magazine photos. As was the case with most press cars in those days, this one was loaded to the gills with options, even though the Superbee (and its corporate cousin Road Runner) were billed as no-frills economy supercars.

In '68, the 426 Street Hemi was rated at 425 horsepower at 5,000 rpm and 490 lb-ft of torque at 4,000 rpm. The rest of the 'Bee's powertrain consisted of an A727 three-speed, a column-shifted TorqueFlite automatic, and a 3.23 Sure Grip rear axle. It had front discs, heavy-duty front torsion bars, rear leaf springs and shocks—all part of the standard Street Hemi

Success on track had given Chrysler's Hemi engines massive cache on the street, so while the stock Street Hemi engine didn't win a lot of stoplight drag races, stories about it did sell magazines.

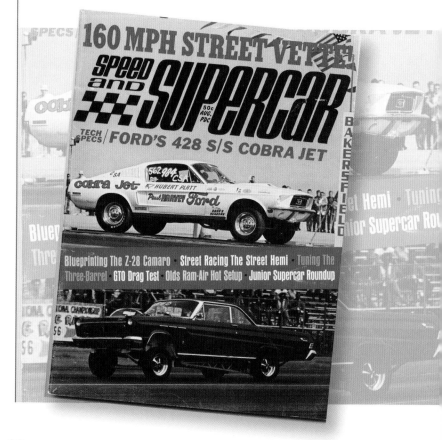

The Superbee was Dodge's answer to sister Chrysler division Plymouth's wildly popular Road Runner.

package—and an optional deluxe all-vinyl bench interior—a definite upgrade from the taxicab standard interior fitted to most Superbees. And this 'Bee seemed to have been screwed together pretty well— no loose pieces of plastic hanging off, no carpeting pulling loose.

As I've stated several times, I wasn't much of a fan of the 426 Street Hemi engine in those days—too much carburetion and too-large ports and valves for good torque on the street. But this one seemed to run well. So a couple of days later, I was ready to hit the streets of Brooklyn and Queens, looking for a run.

As was my usual routine, the first stop was Cross Bay Boulevard in Queens, New York. No one was in the Big Bow-Wow parking lot, so I went straight to Pizza City. It was also quiet. I parked near the front entrance so the bad yellow Superbee was clearly visible from the Cross Bay roadway.

After a few minutes, a guy in a jacked-up, primed '55 Chevy with no front bumper pulled in and parked next to me. Our windows rolled down.

"Looking for a run?" he asked.

"Yeah. What are you running?" I replied.

"No man. Not me. But everybody's over at the Clearview tonight. You'll find plenty of action over there."

With that, I was gone, over to the Clearview.

That's the Clearview Expressway near the Union Turnpike exit, which had become a very switched-on

The Hemi engine's lack of low-rpm torque combined with the ridiculously tall 3.23 rear axle gearing meant that most of the competition handed Oldham his ass when he went street racing in the Hemi Super Bee from a dead stop.

place for street action once the police effectively closed down the Connecting Highway. I cruised into the pits, which meant under the bridge on Union Turnpike. It was crowded and actually tough to find a parking spot. Everybody was there. I got out and watched the migration of bodies over to the new '68 Superbee. There were lots of looks and stares and approvals. A bunch of old pals came over to chat about the Superbee. How did it run? How long did I have it for? What gears did it have? You know, car stuff.

And I got runs, lots of runs. That night, and the next few nights that followed, the Superbee was a good-running, but typical, 426 Street Hemi car. It had almost no low-end torque, a condition amplified by the numerically low and almost laughably conservative 3.23 rear axle gearing. So while I did lots of

The "Bee" in "Superbee" refers to B-body, Chrysler's internal code for its midsized chassis.

street racing with this Dodge Superbee, it was successful only when I ran guys from a roll—say, from 20 mph up. From a dig, I got slaughtered by all the 3.90-geared GTOs, 4.10-geared 440 Mopars, and 3.89-geared Mustangs, not to mention any Corvette and various Buick GSs, Olds 442s, and even an 390 AMC Javelin with 3.91s.

But all these cars fell to the mighty Hemi once the revs were up, we were rolling, the 426 cubes could breathe through the sewer-size ports, and all eight huge barrels of carburetion opened up.

I never took this car to the track for any formal testing, so I can't tell you what it ran in the quarter mile or what its trap speeds were or how well it hauled down in a braking test from 60 mph.

But all in all, it was a very good week in this Dodge Superbee. Hey, this was my job. I had to put up with it. And someone else was even paying for the tires.

1969 Pontiac Firebird 400 Ram Air IV (One of 157)

Back in the day, all I had to do was make a phone call and some cool car would show up, at which point I would run the wheels off of it. But sometimes, I even amazed myself. How did I ever have the balls to pull off some of the scams I worked back then? Of course, I classify them as scams. But the public relations guys I worked with at the car companies figured they were getting it over on me. After all, I was calling them and offering to drive their cars and give their cars free publicity. All they had to do was supply me with the car.

The ultimate deal of all, though, was the '69 Firebird. Not only did I ask old pal Jim Wangers,

Jim Wangers was known for going the extra mile when having Royal Pontiac prep a Pontiac for a magazine test. The performance of the Firebird indicated that Wangers had Milt Schornack, Royal Pontiac's high-performance manager, do it up right.

Pontiac's performance promotion guru, for a new '69 Firebird with the 400 Ram Air IV engine, but also I asked him if I could keep it not for the usual week but for a full month. Not only that, but I asked Wangers to have the engine fully blueprinted and set up at Royal Pontiac. Not only that, but I also specified a close-ratio four-speed trans and 3.90 Safe-T-Track rear. And lastly, if all that that wasn't enough, I asked him to send me a set of mounted up slicks with the car.

Amagingly, Wangers, today known worldwide as the Godfather of the GTO and a major figure in the collector car hobby, said yes to all my shameless, brazen, selfish, insane requests. If your proposal made some sense and would result in positive publicity for Pontiac, he usually did say yes.

About four weeks later, Milt Schornack was on the phone. Schornack was the high-performance manager at Royal Pontiac in Royal Oak, Michigan. Then, Royal was the country's premier high-performance Pontiac dealership, and both Pontiac Motor Division and Wangers used the place as a quasi-factory race shop, not only to build race cars but also to set up special cars for magazine road tests. All of this was

It's fitting that Oldham's test of the Royal Bobcat Pontiac Firebird 400 Ram Air IV appeared in an issue with a 427 Corvette on the cover, since the only car to beat the Firebird in a street race was a 427 Corvette.

highly illegal for Pontiac to do on its own, as there was a GM corporate racing ban in effect at the time. Royal Pontiac was the loophole.

Schornack wanted me to know that the car was ready, on its way, and would arrive in New York City on Friday night.

"Be in front of the New York Coliseum garage about 7 p.m.," Schornack said.

I was standing there at 7 p.m., and sure enough, up drives a bright orange Carousel Red Firebird with Michigan manufacturer plates, the hood scoops sporting little "400" emblems and the doors showing "Royal Bobcat" plaques. Little did I know then that it was one of only 157 Ram Air IV Firebirds that would be built in 1969. The car stopped. The driver got out.

"Are you Joe Oldham?"

"Yeah."

"OK. It's all yours," he said. He handed me the keys and walked away. He didn't ask for any ID. He didn't say anything about the car. He just walked away.

As I watched him disappear into the Manhattan night, I climbed into the car and looked around. There were two M&H street slicks mounted on Rally II wheels in plastic bags in the back seat. Yes! I cranked it up and started the drive home.

On the way, I immediately knew this car had street racing potential. I could feel the responsiveness. This was no ordinary 400-cubic-inch Pontiac smog-motor sitting under the hood, I thought as I powershifted second gear going down Second Avenue. And there it was—the satisfying screech of rubber, lots of rubber, going into second gear.

This was the Ram Air IV 400 engine, officially and conservatively rated at 345 horsepower at 5,400 rpm and 430 lb-ft of torque at 3,700 rpm. But it felt like a bunch more. Compression ratio was 10.75 to 1, and carburetion was a single four-barrel Quadrajet sitting on an aluminum intake manifold. Cam was the 308/320 stick, the most potent hydraulic cam ever in a Pontiac, and the whole thing breathed through two functional hood scoops and a special air cleaner.

With quarter-mile times that were consistently in the mid-13-second range, the Ram Air IV version of the Firebird 400 was one of the fastest cars on the road.

The Graduate.

We'll grant you two wheels are better than none. But look what happens when Firebird swoops onto the scene. If it's our 400 version. You won't believe how this one handles. Don't let the smoothness fool you. New rear axle, new load rates on our multi-leaf rear springs and a set of sticky wide-ovals (mounted on 7-inch rims) put new shine on Firebird's cornering reputation. A 400-cubic-inch, Quadra-jet V-8 attached to a 3-speed, heavy-duty transmission, stirred by a Hurst, is your standard power setup. But there's also our two-scoop Ram Air IV that you can order with a 4-speed hand shifter or with 3-speed Turbo Hydra-matic, if you just tell your dealer.

Obviously, all that genius is below decks. Topside, Firebird comes on with all-new looks. Inside, new comfort. With wider, more heavily padded bucket seats wrapped in Pontiac's own woven vinyl. Also, an all-new highly readable instrument panel.

Hood tach, front disc brakes, variable-ratio power steering, polyglas-cord, wide-tread rubber . . . all that great Pontiac stuff . . . will practically let you build your own Firebird . . . if you want to. And that's a liberal education in itself.

Firebird 400 by Pontiac

Wangers was no fool. He knew that a contented, happy, comfortable journalist wrote more favorable things than a journalist who was uncomfortable. So, in addition to all the hot hardware under the hood, he had packed in the deluxe interior, power front disc brakes, power steering, tilt steering column, Pontiac's best AM-FM stereo, hood tach, Rally II wheels, and a bunch of other stuff.

Since this was to be a long-term test, as opposed to the usual one-week-with-a-test-car routine, I took my time and simply enjoyed the normal ownership experience. I literally just drove it around for a few days, which was a joy in itself because of the sheer responsiveness of the package and the usual attention to detail in the Firebird's interior. Everything felt first rate and was, including the build quality.

The unusual amount of torque on hand made driving the car effortless, and I hardly had to use the excellent Hurst shifter for the four-speed, there being enough torque in just about any situation to merely tip in a little more throttle. Top-gear acceleration was as

strong as first gear in many other cars, thanks to the stiff 3.90 rear axle gearing.

On a cool but sunny Saturday, we took the car out to Suffolk County Raceway in Westhampton, New York, to do a little drag racing and get some accurate acceleration times.

The stock Goodyear F70-14 fiberglass belted white stripe tires quickly proved impossible, simply smoking away at the drop of a clutch. We switched to the big M&Hs and tried a few runs at 20 psi. The strong 400 had enough torque to ripple the sidewalls, but the Firebird was still a handful coming off the line. On every run, the car fishtailed sideways, requiring some steering correction to keep it straight.

My notes for the day indicate that the car was consistently in the mid- to high 13s at 103–107 mph with an absolute best run of 13.54 seconds at 107.02 mph. There was an old, abandoned oval at the Westhampton

Here's some gratuitous tire-destroying porn. This is, after all, what muscle cars are all about.

track that I often used for handling evaluation. Back on the street tires, this Firebird was impressive. I thought the comfortable ride motions would translate into sloppy track handling. Not so. I tended to overdrive the car, entering corners way too fast and too far over my head. Fortunately, the Firebird had a most forgiving suspension. Cornering was on the flat side, with a minimum of pitch and roll. Some traces of understeer were present, but I was able to powerslide the car at will by just feeding in torque with my right foot.

OK, the urge had come. Let's go street racing.

I did the usual Connecting Highway to Cross Bay Boulevard cruise one night, had a few runs, and took out a few GTOs and SS-396 Chevelles. The Firebird 400 was a real sleeper. Firebirds were rare those days on the street racing scene, and those that were around didn't run very well. So our orange Bird was an unexpected Q-ship. Ram Air IV Pontiacs, in general, were few and far between, and anything short of a Ram Air IV spent most of the night looking up the back of some other guy's dual exhausts.

This Firebird was different. It was hot, and I won just about every run I picked up. It took a 427 Corvette to take out the mighty Royal Bobcat Firebird 400.

By the following Saturday night, the word was out: Don't fuck with the orange Firebird. Don't run it for money, and don't run it at all unless you got a really mean machine. The pits down Cross Bay were loaded by the time I pulled in at midnight. Everyone had heard we were coming. Everyone wanted to look under the hood. I obliged.

They couldn't see anything except the foam air cleaner that sealed up against the hood to create the ram air effect and that single four-barrel carb. This perplexed the hotshoes even more. This was just a stock Firebird 400?

Not much really happened that night and, in the coming weeks, it was tough to get a run, any run. I cruised, but they all declined, and that was it for the rest of the month. No one would come near the Firebird after that, for good reason.

This Royal Bobcat Firebird 400 Ram Air IV will go down in my personal history as one of the hottest muscle cars I ever drove. It was a true multipurpose car that you could drive to work on Friday, street race on Saturday night, and win at the drags on Sunday.

1969 Dodge Charger 500 (One of 15 or 27)

Even in the day, a '69 Dodge Charger 500 was a rare animal. And no wonder. According to Mopar numbers guru Galen Govier, Ma Mopar made only 580

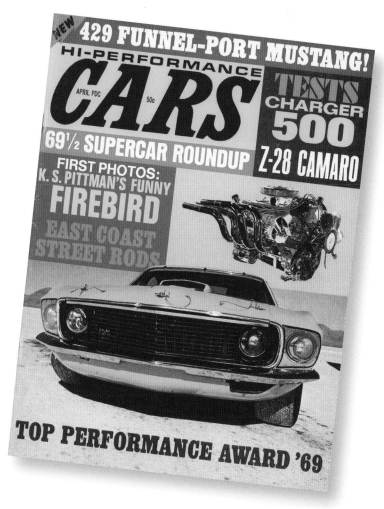

The Charger 500's sole reason for being was to homologate the car for NASCAR racing. Dodge needed to build 500 of them, and it built just 580.

of them in that one model year (subsequent year Charger 500s were merely a trim level in the Charger line and had none of the body modifications of the '69). Of those 580 cars, Govier says just 120 of them were packed with the 426 Hemi engine. Of those 120, other sources say only about 15 (or 27) had a four-speed manual trans.

I knew absolutely none of this on the day in November 1968 when the phone rang in my cubicle at *Hi-Performance Cars* magazine. It was Moon Mullins, the Dodge public relations guy in New York, offering me a new Hemi four-speed Charger 500 for the weekend. Did I want it? Did I want to bang Brigitte Bardot?

This was a great deal. A Hemi four-speed Dodge Charger 500 for a weekend of street racing, and I didn't even have to do any actual work writing about

it. Perfect. As it turned out, not only was the weekend of street racing a total bust, but I hardly got any seat time at all in this car, one of 15 (or 27) ever built.

When Moon hung up, I looked up the press release we had received on the Charger 500. On September 1, 1968, Dodge announced that it had contracted with Creative Industries of Detroit to hand-build at least five hundred examples of a special model Charger to make it eligible for the 1969 NASCAR season—five hundred being the number of units NASCAR considered "production." The cars would all have the 426 Street Hemi engine rated at

Dodge gave the Charger 500 aerodynamic tricks like a flush-mounted grille and rear window to help it dominate on NASCAR's super speedways, but it wasn't enough, and Ford ate Dodge's lunch with its aerodynamic specials.

Unlike the Hemi Superbee Oldham had tested the previous year, the Hemi Charger 500 came with proper gearing: a Dana 60 with 4.10 gears, making it a much stronger performer. Unfortunately, the NYPD was cracking down on street racing at the time, and Oldham never got the opportunity to turn a wheel in anger.

425 horsepower as standard equipment and were to be modified with a flush-mounted front grille, flush-mounted rear backlite and other details, all in the name of aerodynamics.

In retrospect, the Charger 500 program was a total failure for Chrysler. Most of these cars were built not with the Hemi but with the much cheaper and simpler 440 four-barrel engine to make them more affordable. The aerodynamic changes to the Charger's body proved to be not enough against Ford's "aero" twins, the Torino Talladega and Mercury Cyclone Spoiler. Later in '69, Chrysler countered with the Dodge Daytona and Plymouth Superbird "wing" cars, and you know the rest of the story.

On Friday, I worked late to let some of the NYC traffic wind down. About 8 p.m., I made my way over

to the garage on East 43rd Street where Chrysler kept its press cars. I signed all the paperwork, and the attendant pointed to a bronze Charger over in a corner.

There it was—one of 15 (or 27), although I had no clue at that moment. The flush-mounted grille definitely gave the car a distinctive look, and the way they had taken the tunneled back glass out of the sailpanels and mounted it flush with the edges was pretty amazing.

Inside, the car had buckets, a console, and a neat four-speed Hurst shifter with a big, round, wood-grained knob on the end. The elephantine 426 Street Hemi under the hood had twin four-barrel carbs sitting under a chrome air cleaner. A rated 425 horses

The street version of the Charger 500 came with a few more amenities than its racing brethren. The example Oldham tested is among the rarest of the rare because it was one of only a handful equipped with a Hemi engine and a four-speed transmission.

the inevitable police crackdown. But this was three weeks later. I hoped it was enough time for things to blow over.

It wasn't. I cruised Cross Bay from one end to the other. Twice. I parked in the Pizza City and Big Bow-Wow parking lots, waiting. Nothing. I was in the vicinity of Nassau Expressway, so I made a pass. Nothing. I drove past the parking areas of Union Turnpike. Nothing.

By this time, it was around midnight. If anything was happening, it would be happening at the Connecting Highway. I drove up there, but the crackdown had extended even to the Connecting. Both elevated service roads were deserted—except for four NYPD Plymouth cruisers, two on each side, just parked there, waiting. The Mopars win again. I went home. Surely, Saturday night would be much, much better.

Only 120 Charger 500s came equipped with the infamous Hemi engine. Oldham describes the shrieking sound of all eight carburetor barrels opening up and dumping gallons of high-octane gas into the combustion chambers as "shocking."

awaited my right foot. The distinctive Mopar starter whine preceded the Hemi's throaty gurgle as the engine fired and we were off.

New York City traffic was New York City traffic, even at this late hour. I slogged through to the Queens Midtown Tunnel, acquainting myself with the clutch, shifter feel, and gauges. Once through the tunnel and out onto the Long Island Expressway, I gave it a few blasts—some in fourth gear, then a few downshifted to third. Opening up all eight barrels made almost a shocking air-shrieking sound as though the hood itself was being sucked into the carburetors. Nice.

The heck with dinner. Time was a-wasting. I exited the Long Island Expressway at Woodhaven Boulevard and drove south to Cross Bay Boulevard. Cross Bay, a notorious street-racing venue, had been pretty much shut down by the NYPD a few weeks before. Some asswipe had lost control of his car in a residential area, and the NYC tabloids had said he was street racing. The ensuing public outcry brought

On the way home, I stopped on a deserted street I knew with cemeteries on both sides. I had to give this beast a blast before putting it to bed. I revved to 4,000, dropped the clutch hard, and hung on. The 4.10 Dana 60 gears inside the Super Track Pack axle bit, and the F70-15 fiberglass belted Goodyears went up in smoke. At 5,000 rpm, I slammed a massive second gear, catching maybe 40 feet of rubber. Third was a blind rush, and then I was out of room. A nice ending to a frustrating evening, and there was always tomorrow.

I awoke Saturday morning to a heavy rain washing over New York City. It rained the whole day and night, and there was obviously no street racing to be had. I didn't even take the Charger 500 out.

Sunday was always a no-action day in New York City street racing, so I didn't even bother. I shot a few photos of the Charger in the morning, then watched the late game as the New York Jets crushed the Boston Patriots. *The Ed Sullivan Show* featured the Moody Blues, Senor Wences, and a trained seal act.

All told, the Ram Air IV GTO was a very nice, well-balanced car: comfortable, nice-handling, very well-built, and the fastest GTO Oldham had ever tested. But he never took it racing. It's best times were in the low-14-second range, and by 1970, people were street racing cars in such high states of tune they had to be towed to the races because they were virtually undrivable on the street.

Suddenly, it was Monday. I drove the Charger 500 into the city, turned it in at the Chrysler garage, and went to the office deflated. Subsequently, another of our staff editors picked up the same car and wrote it up for *Hi-Performance Cars*. I have never seen another '69 Charger 500.

1970 Pontiac GTO Ram Air IV (One of 627)

Before there was Facebook, MySpace, MyFace, AssBook, Twitter, Shitter, Spitter, and other social networking media, there were magazines. People got their information from printed-on-paper magazines. You went down to your local candy store or newsstand or convenience store, looked over the selection of magazines, and chose one or more for purchase. If you were like me, they were mostly car magazines with maybe an occasional motorcycle publication thrown in.

Magazines were purchased based on the consumer's reaction to the cover photo and the cover lines of type, called blurbs. Blurbs were meant to inform, shock, surprise, delight, and otherwise engage the reader and hopefully entice him to buy. Newsstand sales were extremely important to magazines. If your newsstand numbers were down, you might be out of a job. If you worked for a magazine, as I did back in the day, part of your job was to dream up enticing cover lines to help the newsstand sale.

So it was one day in 1970 that I walked into the office of the boss, Marty Schorr, editorial director of *Hi-Performance Cars* and all the other car books published by Magnum-Royal Publications in New York City.

"Marty, I have a great cover line."

"Good. What is it?"

875 HP 454 CHEVY!

HI-PERFORMANCE

CARS

JULY PDC 50c

Preview: INDY 500

MIKE MITCHELL, WORLD'S FASTEST HIPPIE

RAM AIR GTO TEST · ENGINE BLUEPRINTING
STREET RACING SCENE · DUNE BUGGYS & ATVs
HOT CHEVY SETUPS · SO-CAL SUPER DRAGS

"Utimate Shootout: GTO vs. GTX," I said.

"Great line," he said. "Jack that thing up and shove an article under it—for the next issue," he said.

Just like that, I had my next assignment.

It went like that sometimes. Sometimes, you invented the cover blurb before you even had the article. Other times, it was the other way around.

So "GTO vs. GTX" was the reason I found myself driving around in a brand-new, one-of-627-ever-built 1970 Pontiac GTO Ram Air IV four-speed hardtop.

Pontiac had sent us the car several weeks before the actual shootout took place. The GTX was delayed in arriving in NYC, so we spent lots of time with the GTO. So much time, in fact, that we were able to do a couple of separate stories on this car, plus the shootout later on.

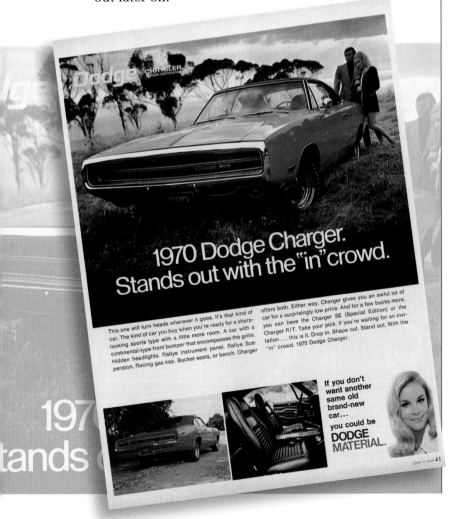

I had asked Pontiac to send us the hottest GTO they made for 1970, knowing it would be pitted against a 426 Hemi-powered Plymouth GTX. I expected them to send us a new-for-1970 455 HO–powered car rated at 360 horsepower (370 in the Grand Prix) with 500 lb-ft of torque. Instead, they shipped in a GTO packing the holdover 400-cubic-inch Ram Air IV engine, which Pontiac still considered the hottest car they built.

It was quickly evident to me that this was, by far, the best-running GTO I had driven in years, perhaps ever. In '68, I had purchased new a GTO 400 HO four-speed car. They never ran side by side, but if they had, I can tell you that the '70 test car would have blown my '68 so far into the weeds it would have been featured on an episode of the ABC TV show *Missing*. There was no question that the '70 Ram Air IV GTO was one of the quickest and fastest production, off-the-showroom-floor cars that the guys at Pontiac ever screwed together.

That's not to say it was one of the quickest and fastest cars of 1970. It wasn't. Its competitors had long ago passed the performance levels of this GTO. Still, you had to admire the engineering that went into this engine.

The special Ram Air IV 400 engine block had four-bolt main bearings to take the extra thrashing Pontiac engineers knew this engine would be subjected to. The camshaft was the wildest ever stuffed into a Pontiac block—308 degrees intake duration, 320 degrees exhaust duration, 87 degrees overlap, and 0.527-in. lift on both intake and exhaust valves. And the cam was not shy about making itself known at idle. This thing had a lope.

Carburetion was by one Rochester Quadrajet carb on a cast-iron intake manifold. Cold air was ducted through functional hood scoops. Not as sexy as a tri-power setup but actually more efficient.

The biggest change of all compared to other Pontiac 400-cubic-inch engines was the

The Ram Air IV package was an impressive piece of engineering, featuring heads with huge round ports and exhaust manifolds that were as efficient as many race headers.

cylinder heads. If there was any secret to the success of the Ram Air IV engine, it was exhaust breathing. The RA IV heads featured huge round exhaust ports that were 36 percent larger in area and featured a much straighter shot, clear out of the valve, than previous head designs. Also, the two center exhaust ports were no longer siamesed into one large manifold port as on previous designs.

The other special goodie on the Ram Air IV was the very streamlined, high-flow exhaust manifolds. They were, in fact, just as efficient as aftermarket high-flow tubular exhaust manifolds but weighed more. Forged pistons, lightweight valvetrain components that allowed a 6,400 rpm shift point, and new calibrations for the ignition system and Quadrajet carb also added horsepower to the Ram Air IV.

It was all topped off with chrome valve covers and a chrome air cleaner and oil cap. You just don't see beautiful engines like this today, now that a sheet of plastic covers everything under the hood. The Ram Air IV for 1970 carried a factory rating of 370 horsepower at 5,500 rpm and 445 lb-ft of torque at 3,900 rpm. It all resided on the dealer order blank as Option Code 347 and cost you $558.20

extra when you ordered it on your new 1970 GTO.

Right there is one of the main reasons Pontiac built so few of them in 1970: $550 was a lot of extra money for an engine option. The other reason is that although this was the fastest Pontiac for 1970, it still crapped out on the street compared to its supercar competitors.

My test car had the four-speed close-ratio Muncie transmission, a 3.90 rear axle ratio with Safe-T-Track limited slip differential, 14x6 Rally II wheels, Uniroyal G70-14 Tiger Paw white lettered tires, Option Code 621 ride and handling suspension (for $4.21 extra!), a console, an AM-FM radio, gauges, and other comfort and convenience items.

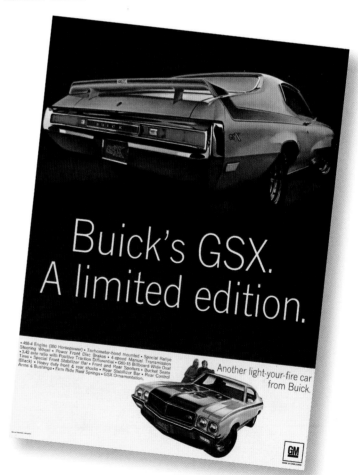

Base price of a '70 GTO hardtop was $3,267. This test car listed for $4,948—obviously a loaded car. Curb weight of my test car was a tubby 3,897 pounds.

On a cool Saturday in March, I took the car to Suffolk County Raceway in Westhampton, New York, to check the numbers. I was flatly disappointed.

Runs started in the 14.60s with trap speeds around 98 mph. But the times improved with every pass, dropping to a low of 14.14 seconds with a best trap speed of 102.50 mph. My notes from the day are revealing. The car just would not ET, and I had severe traction problems with the stock G70-14 fiberglass-belted Uniroyals. No doubt drag slicks or a modern radial tire would have knocked mountains off my ETs that day. But I had neither with me, so it was a moot point.

I drove the GTO very hard during the test session, trying all kinds of off-the-line and shifting techniques, including full-bore powershifts at 6,500 rpm with my right foot flat to the floor. The Muncie shifted like all Muncies—like the proverbial hot knife through soft butter. I got the best times shifting hard at 6,000 rpm, not 6,500. Still, this was the best I, or anyone else at the track with me that day, could do. It was painfully obvious the Ram Air IV wanted slicks and open exhausts, as did all race engines.

Overall handling was pretty good. This was due, finally, to Pontiac engineers going to a rear anti-roll stabilizer bar, something Oldsmobile 442s had had since 1964. The GTO understeered slightly but never felt as if it was pushing out the front end too hard—as many of the muscle cars of the day did do. The rear sway bar helped a great deal and reduced body roll in corners too. In fact, the limiting factor to the GTO's

As impressive as the Ram Air IV was, by 1970, when competitors were running 440-, 454-, and 455-cubic-inch engines, 400 cubic inches no longer cut it.

handling prowess was the car's tire/wheel combo.

Not only were Pontiac engineers six years behind in discovering the positive points of the rear anti-roll bar, but they were way behind in tires and wheels too, which was surprising because Pontiac had previously been a leader in that area. Where the leading muscle cars of the day were shod with 15x7 wheels mounting fat G60-15 tires, Pontiac was still poking along with the old G70-14 tires on 14x6 wheels, a decidedly played-out combination. The following year, Pontiac did go to the more modern G60 tires on 15-inch wheels as an option.

The interior was almost plush, very comfortable, and well finished. The dash had all the gauges in perfect position, and the whole interior was almost dead quiet and rather classy. The whole car was put together with the care and quality that was typical of General Motors products in 1970.

By 1970, the GTO was a mature muscle car, having already been in existence for seven model

American Motors and Mark Donohue specially prepared and modified the new Javelin-AMX, so you don't have to.

Last season, in Trans-Am Road Racing, Mark Donohue was racing for us and winning.

Obviously, we were thrilled. We had never won in Trans-Am before. And that gave us an idea.

Why not ask Donohue to take some of his special preparations and modifications for the track, and incorporate them into a Javelin for the road.

And that's what he did.

The new Javelin-AMX is a completely redesigned performance car. From its fast, glacial slopes on the outside. To its cockpit console on the inside.

But first and foremost, as a true performance car, it is built around the principle that air pressure has to work for you. Not against you.

It has a body that is wider and lower on the outside. With a wider rear tread for better stability.

It has a front wire-mesh grille screen that is flush with the wind.

A rear spoiler specially designed by Donohue.

New intake manifolds for deeper breathing. New exhaust manifolds to reduce back pressure. A new optional cowl-air induction system. And an optional front spoiler.

Of course, the new Javelin-AMX also has everything else you'd normally expect on a performance car.

A standard 360 CID V-8 engine that develops 245 horsepower. Or an optional 4 barrel carb for 285 horsepower.

A standard 3-speed all synchromesh floor shift transmission with an 11" heavy duty clutch. Or an optional 4-speed with a Hurst shifter.

An optional heavy duty suspension system, big tach, and gauges. Standard fat Polyglas™ tires, mag style wheels, and a couple of things you wouldn't expect.

New optional ventilated-rotor front disc brakes to fight brake fade. And a new optional 401 CID engine that generates 330 horsepower.

Mark Donohue will be driving the new Javelin-AMX in next season's Trans-Am.

You could be driving it right now.

If you had to compete with GM, Ford and Chrysler, what would you do?
◢ American Motors

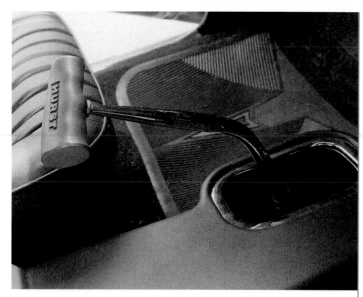

The Hurst shifter made rowing through the giant gears in the transmission a much easier task.

years. As such, Pontiac had the time to sort out all the irregularities and rough edges, and our test car showed it. But with that class and quality had come complacency. The behind-the-curve thinking on the wheels and tires and suspension were problematic, as was the lack of horsepower and torque in a day when 454 and 455 was the norm. Yes, Pontiac offered a 455 in the GTO, but it never ran with the likes of LS6 Chevelles, 455 Stage 1 Buicks, Olds 455 W-30s, 440 6-Pack Mopars, and other cars of that ilk.

This is one of the only cars I ever tested during that golden era of the muscle car that I did not take street racing. Here's why.

By the spring of 1970, when I had this car in my possession, the street racing scene in the New York area had become so wild that there simply was no point in running a bone-stock 400-cube GTO. The year 1970 was arguably the pinnacle of the muscle car era, and you had to have big inches to be competitive on the street, preferably *worked* inches. Hell, some guys were even *towing in* for street racing. If you weren't in that league in 1970, you might as well just stay on the sidelines and watch. While I had the GTO, I just watched.

Today, in retrospect, I can appreciate what a nice ride this GTO was. Back then, it was a relatively wimpy car that had been passed by the rest of the muscle car world.

1970 Buick GSX 455 Stage 1 (One of 282)

Buick's new-for-1970 GS-455 was a fast, beautiful—but conservative—muscle car, a classic that could kick ass on any given Sunday. But conservative. Buick stylists soon fixed that, however. If the marketplace demanded bolder, louder graphics, then by God, Buick would be competitive. More conservative, perhaps, and in better taste, of course. After all, this *was* a Buick. And more expensive, because this was a Buick. But competitive nonetheless.

While John DeLorean stayed the 400-cubic-inch course at Pontiac, over at sister-division Buick, management jumped on the big-inch bandwagon as soon as GM lifted its 400-cubic-inch limit on midsized cars for the 1970 model year and dropped a breathed-on 455-cubic-inch mill into its GSX muscle car.

By 1970, Oldham had grown bored with the over-the-top styling of many muscle cars, but on the Buick GSX, he felt the striping and spoiler worked well together and looked good.

So in the spring of 1970, Buick released the GSX, a trim option on top of the GS-455, one of the most sought-after muscle cars today. Naturally, we wanted to test drive a 455 GSX as soon as it was announced. But we had to wait until the New York Auto Show was over. That's right. The car I test drove was the actual show car on display atop the turntable at the New York Auto Show in April 1970—one of one, if you will. Once the show was over on Monday morning, the Saturn Yellow GSX was removed from the turntable and turned over to me at the New York Coliseum garage.

One other thing that made my test car unique was that it had a 3.64 rear axle ratio rather than the standard 3.42. Originally, the 3.64 ratio was to have been standard in all GSXs, but last-minute problems with emission certification forced Buick engineers to go with the standard 3.42 ratio that came on all Gran Sports.

Exactly what was a GSX, and how did it differ from a regular run-of-the-mill GS-455? It started with a GS-455 and added the A9 option group, which included a hood-mounted tachometer, a special Rallye (their spelling) steering wheel, power front disc brakes, a four-speed manual transmission, a 3.42 rear axle ratio with Positive Traction limited slip differential, the Rallye Ride Control suspension package, front and rear spoilers, a black bucket seat interior, a heavy duty cooling package, a consolette, G60-15 tires on beautiful 15x7 chrome road wheels,

Though rated at just 360 horsepower, the mighty Stage I version of Buick's 455-cubic-inch engine was rated at 510 lb-ft of torque. The GSX was the fastest Buick Oldham ever tested, though he was unable to get hard numbers because of timing equipment failure at the drag strip.

The GSX was easily the most opulent car of the entire muscle-car era.

Rallye instrumentation, GSX ornamentation, and a custom interior package. All this cost you $1,195.87 over the price of a GS-455, which stickered at $3,283.

Except for the ornamentation, you could order any of this equipment on any regular GS-455, so you had to really want the GSX look to pay for it. In retrospect, not many buyers went for it, and the GSX turned out to be one of the rarest of all muscle cars. In fact, just 678 GSX hardtops were made in 1970, 278 with the regular 455 and 400 with the Stage 1 engine package. Of the 400 Stage 1 cars, my test car was one of 282 made with the Turbo 400 automatic, with 118 packing the four-speed.

My test car had many options. The first, and most important, was the dynamite Stage 1 engine option for the 455 engine. It listed for an extra $113.75 when ordered on a GSX-equipped car, $157.43 on any other GS. Rated at a conservative 360 horsepower at 4,600 rpm and a tremendous 510 lb-ft of torque at 2,800 rpm, this engine stands at the pinnacle of Buick performance. No Buick before or since has ever packed more power.

The car also had the Turbo Hydra-Matic 400 automatic transmission, a $42.24 option over the standard four-speed manual. A full-length console replaced the stubby consolette for $24.23 extra. Fast variable ratio power steering ($121.12), push-button AM radio ($69.51), and tinted glass ($26.33) were other extras on the test car. With a $56 destination charge, the sticker for my no-air GSX tester was $4,932.05. I recently saw a similar car cross the auction block for $155,000.

One of the side benefits of the GSX package is that it made a GS-455 the best handling of any muscle car I had ever driven to that point. My notes from 1970 say so, and I remember opening my original article with that statement. The suspension engineers simply found the exact right combination of ride and handling. There was certainly nothing exotic under the car, just the perfect combination of springs, shocks, anti-roll stabilizer bars, wheels, and tires you could get on a GM A-body. Huge (for the time) G60-15 Goodyear Polyglas GT tires were the biggest and best you could get on any American car in 1970. The age of the radial tire, though, was about to dawn.

This was also the first year that GM made widespread use of rear anti-roll stabilizer bars on their cars. Previously, only Oldsmobile 442s had them. In 1970, the bars spread to Buicks, Pontiacs, and Chevys. As such, my test GSX had one, and combined with the big tires and stiffer springs and shocks, it made for a truly impressive ride and handling combination.

I was never a fan of the gaudy GTO Judge/Ford Torino Cobra school of tape-and-decals graphics packages, but I admit that, as they go, the GSX was one of the best scoops-and-spoiler treatments out of Detroit. For one thing, the rear spoiler wasn't some freaky-looking Italian salami slicer pasted on as an afterthought. The GSX's spoiler looked as though it belonged there, and the stripes blended very well with the rest of the car's bodylines. It was tasteful in the Buick tradition.

As in most Buicks of the day, the interior of my test car was sumptuous. The black interior and black padded steering wheel were sporty but luxurious. Steering was quick and precise thanks to the variable ratio engineering. Over the road with the windows up, my notes say that the car was dead silent despite

In addition to being the most luxurious muscle car Oldham tested, the GSX was also the best handling of the breed.

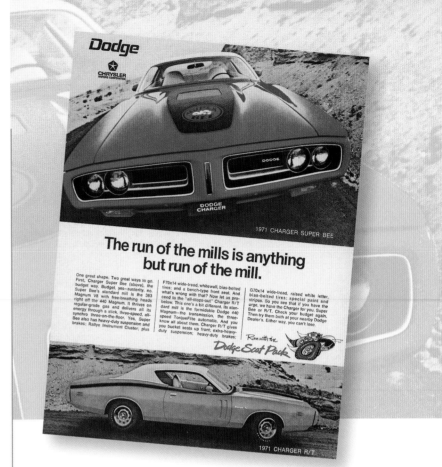

the 455 cubes throbbing under the hood. Only under full throttle with all four bores of the Rochester Quadrajet opened wide was there any noise at all, and that noise was the comforting sound of many cubic feet of air rushing through the carb and into the engine.

With the 3.64 ratio, the road cruising wasn't bad—or so it seemed then. At 60 mph, the engine was turning 2,800 rpm, right at the torque peak for instant passing power. Of course, today, with built-in overdrive, many cars are almost idling at 60 on the highway, turning maybe 1,500 rpm. Put a non-car person into a GSX on a highway at 60 mph today, and he would think the car was a bomb ready to explode.

But interior comfort and quietness was but a passing curiosity in a car like a GSX 455 Stage 1. You want to know how it did on the drag strip and on the street, right?

With its Saturn yellow paint and cheese grater rear spoiler, the GSX was as distinctive-looking as it was luxurious and capable.

First, the street.

I cruised most of the New York street racing scenes that were operating back then. The car caused a small sensation wherever it went, being the only GSX in existence at that point in time. My notes indicate that the car felt explosive off the line in light-to-light confrontations, and I had several interesting moments with the car.

I can remember blowing off the likes of GTOs and 442s in informal sessions late at night on deserted stretches of Cross Bay Boulevard in Queens. But frankly, I couldn't get many runs in the car. Remember, I was driving around in a show car. Most

guys had not even heard of the GSX and weren't about to risk reputation with girlfriends and guyfriends to take on an unknown quantity painted in chrome yellow with black racing stripes all over it. The rumbling idle of the Stage 1 engine didn't exactly help potential opponents in the self-confidence area. As such, my week on the street with the GSX was fairly dull and routine. A solid-lifter big block Camaro did wipe me out one night on Cross Bay.

I never had the chance to run this car against the clocks on a drag strip. I did take it to Raceway Park one day for a photo session, but the clocks were not set up, and we did not record any actual times for the car.

At Englishtown, the stock tires gave it their best shot off the line, but it was easy to break them loose for smoky burnout shots. I did make a few full-track runs with no clocks and could tell that easing off the line, then mashing it, was the quick way to quick times. I estimate that the car ran 14 seconds flat at 103 mph. No doubt modern radials would have put this car into the 13s, which we proved many years later for a story in *Popular Mechanics* where we ran old muscle cars with modern tires. The GS-455 we had that day ran deep into the 13s.

No question, a Stage 1 Buick is one of the quickest, best-running muscle cars of all time. I was lucky to get to drive the first one on the road, anywhere. It was loud without actually yelling, but to muscle car enthusiasts, it still speaks volumes.

1971 429 SCJ Ford Torino Cobra (One of 199)

Up until the 1968 model year, Ford was a loser on the street. Yes, it had proven its mettle on road racing tracks and high-banked ovals, but on the street, it was an effeminate pansy of a car that regularly got bullied and beat up by the big guys. Finally, the '68 1/2 428 Cobra Jet–powered Mustang salvaged some self-esteem for Ford. Previous to the '68 1/2 428CJ Mustang, Fords regularly got their ass kicked in and punched out.

The Ford product planners knew all this and knew they had left a lot of money on the table by not having competitive products to offer to street performance enthusiasts throughout the heyday of muscle cars.

In 1970, the hot 429 Cobra Jet engine made its appearance along with the 429 Super Cobra Jet option. Once again, Ford had the hardware but couldn't get it into their street cars. Very few solid-lifter 429 Super Cobra Jet optioned cars were built, although regular 429 Cobra Jet–powered cars were fairly plentiful at Ford dealerships.

There were other problems. Ford's muscle car packaging was confusing to buyers. Its prime muscle car was called the Torino Cobra. Its engines were called Cobra Jets and Super Cobra Jets. You could get a Cobra Jet engine in a Cobra. Or was that a Cobra in a Super Cobra Jet?

Sadly, Ford never really got its muscle-car act together.

It's too bad because from 1968 on, Ford had one of the better muscle-car products. A prime example was a '71 429SCJ Torino Cobra I tested in the fall of 1970.

When I went to the United Nations Apartments Parking Garage on East 49th Street in Manhattan, where Ford kept its press fleet cars, to pick up the

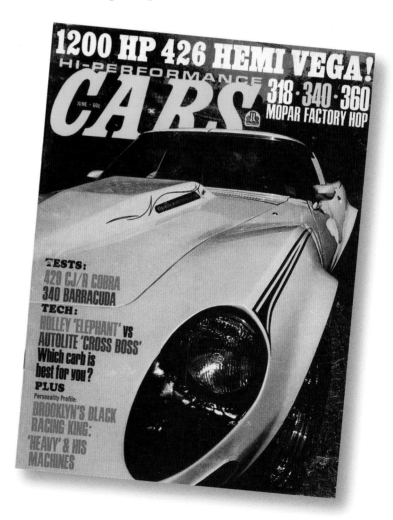

By the time Oldham tested Ford's 429 SCJ Torino Cobra, the original muscle-car era was on its last legs.

test car, my first impression was, "Oh, God." It was bright yellow and had all the garish styling cues and gimmicks that Ford's design department thought muscle-car buyers wanted in 1971. Things like a blacked-out hood, hood pins, scoops, slats on the back window, and lots of other little touches indicated to me that Ford's design department was about two years behind the rest of the industry. By 1971, other Detroit manufacturers had already gone conservative in their approach to muscle cars in deference to the insurance industry's blitz on muscle car rates and the attack on muscle cars in general by the safety freakos.

Oldham was put off by the tape graphics on his test car, but without said graphics, the Torino cut a handsome profile.

Ford, though, was still there with 1969-style garishness and blatant bad taste. While I liked the basic design of the '71 Ford Torino, which was carry-over from 1970 except for a slightly different grille and new emblems, the Cobra option body treatment frankly left me gagging.

Under the hood, it was a different story. I loved this car under the hood. It had the optional—and rare—Super Cobra Jet package, which included solid-lifter camshaft, higher 11.3-to-1 compression forged pistons, a larger 780 cfm Holley four-barrel, a high-rise aluminum intake manifold, and other goodies. The engine was rated at 375 horsepower at 5,600 rpm and 450 lb-ft of torque at 3,400 rpm.

Though muscle cars were already suffering from the detuning of their engines by 1971, the SCJ Torino Cobra was still a wicked-fast car capable of breaking into the 13-second bracket at the drag strip.

Production figures for these cars are hard to come by because Ford never released official production figures, but several Internet sources say that Ford built 37,518 Torino two-door hardtops in 1971. Of those, 3,054 carried the Cobra option. And of those, just 199 carried the R-code 429 Super Cobra Jet solid-lifter engine. Where these sources got these figures I cannot tell you. I, myself, have not seen another '71 R-code 429 Super Cobra Jet Torino.

The rest of the powertrain consisted of Ford's three-speed SelecShift C6 automatic transmission and 3.91 gears with limited slip differential. That was the hottest combination offered by Ford in 1971, although you could have ordered a 4.30 axle ratio had you been so inclined.

On a gray, rainy day, I made my way out to Raceway Park in Englishtown, New Jersey, for our drag strip test session. One pass, and I knew

the Torino Cobra SCJ was a more than respectable performer. In fact, it was a stormer, and the horsepower ratings were extremely conservative and, frankly, meaningless.

With the hot solid-lifter camshaft, the power didn't really come on until the engine climbed up on the cam around 3,000 rpm. Then I could feel the engine pull strongly all through the gears right to 6,000 rpm. By 1971, emission controls had already tightened, and my notes from the test session indicate that the Holley four-barrel was jetted way too lean and the ignition was way retarded, which was par for the day of emission controls on muscle cars. Still, the engine made plenty of horsepower.

With the 3.91 gears and damp pavement, getting off the line was rough. Too much throttle, and the rear tires literally went up in smoke. Not enough, and the poor low-end torque characteristics of the racing cam made the car bog a few feet off the line. Finally, I opted for lots of smoke, figuring that keeping the revs up was a better deal than the bog, and besides,

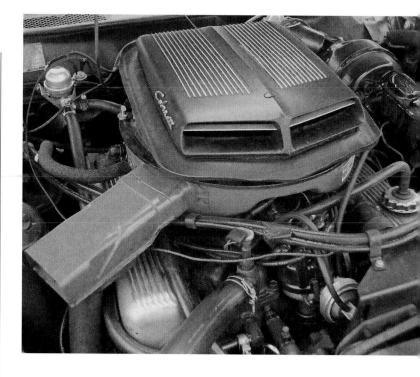

The age of engines being hidden beneath a maze of pollution-control equipment had already arrived in 1971, but at least the SCJ 429 engine had a functioning hood scoop.

it made for better photos. As it turned out, that technique netted us the best performance.

The best timeslip that day at Raceway Park indicated an elapsed time of 13.70 seconds with a best trap speed of 106 mph. Referring to my notes, I was satisfied with that performance but not overjoyed. In retrospect, I may have been driving the quickest and fastest car of 1971.

Despite the tubby 3,800-pound weight, the Torino Cobra got around the Raceway Park handling loop in fairly good fashion. By today's standards, the tires were puny little F70-14 bias-belted wide treads that didn't really help handling. But any 429-powered Ford was automatically equipped with Ford's so-called competition suspension package, which helped tidy up the handling. The ride was rough by today's standards, but the stiffer springs and stabilizer bar helped control body roll in corners. I encountered some roll, though, while powering through, and the car could have used a rear stabilizer

bar, but Ford engineers hadn't yet discovered such a thing. The staggered rear shocks, part of the competition suspension package, did a good job of controlling wheel hop off the line.

Out on the open road, this car came into its own. It was big and heavy and somewhat ponderous on a road course. But all those qualities gave it a tremendously stable feel out on the road at speed. I drove Canada's Highway 401 for hours at speeds over 100 mph—you could do that back then and never see a cop—and never felt unsafe or unstable or uncomfortable in any way.

In retrospect, the '71 Torino Cobra was what Ford should have been producing for the muscle car freaks in 1969. In 1969, it would have been right in the thick of the muscle car sweepstakes, up against the new GTO Judge and stylin' all the way. As it was, by 1971, as good as the Ford Torino Cobra was, that boat had sailed.

Rear window slats were already out of style by 1971, but they did prevent the sun from baking rear-seat passengers.

It was a great muscle car, but the 429 SCJ Torino Cobra arrived at the party too late to make a real impact. Had Ford built such a car three years earlier, it might have gone down as one of the all-time greats.

1971 401 AMC Javelin AMX (One of 745)

American Motors built just 745 401 Javelin/AMXs in 1971, and thank God for that. Here is a car that literally fell apart around us during the two weeks our staff had it. Talk about your lousy cars. This was easily the worst-built muscle car I have ever driven.

The capper was when managing editor Al Root pulled away from a light a few blocks from where he lived in New York City, only to have the car stop dead with a loud *clunk*. He wondered what happened for a few moments, then saw a tire-wheel-brake drum assembly roll slowly away from the right side of the car. The entire assembly had sheared off the right rear axle of the Javelin, which was now sitting on the pavement on the brake shoes. The car was a real piece of shit.

And we said so, in print.

In fact, we printed a photo of the Javelin sitting there on its right rear brake shoes. The article was a collaborative effort of the *Cars* magazine staff. Marty Schorr wrote the text. I tested the car at the track and shot most of the photos, and Root drove the car for a few days, contributing commentary and the infamous busted wheel photo.

The day the issue came out some three months later, the phone rang in the office. It was Gerald C. Meyers, the president of American Motors, and he wanted to talk to me. We were all shocked. No big wheel ever called anyone here at little *Hi-Performance Cars* magazine. We weren't a big powerhouse magazine, like *Car and Driver* or *Motor Trend* or *Hot Rod*, with hundreds of thousands of readers. We were little *Hi-Performance Cars* magazine.

OK, I thought, as I walked to my desk to take the call. What does he want with me? I put in on speaker so we could all hear.

AUG. 1971
60¢
K

14 PAGES CHEVY COMP SETUPS!

HI-PERFORMANCE
CARS

AUG. 1971
60¢
K
47283

DRAG TESTS:
401 AMX
340 DEMON

TECH ANALYSIS:
440 FOUR-WHEEL-DRIVE MOPAR!

COMPETITION
SPECIALS:
A&P Auto—392
HEMI BLUEPRINT
BOOTH/ARONS—PRO STOCK
SUPER CAMARO
KELLY CHADWICK—470-INCH
CHEVY FUEL FUNNY
DICK CHARBONNEAU—RECORD-HOLDING
427 WEDGE WAGON

PLUS

DILBERT FARB WRINGS OUT A MINI-T ROADSTER
TWO-BARREL HOLLEY SETUP FOR 427-454 CHEVYS
HUNTINGTON ON SETTING UP A JR PRO STOCK CLASS

"Hello, this is Joe Oldham," is about all I got out. For the next seven or eight minutes, Gerald C. Meyers, chairman, president, and chief executive officer of American Motors, berated me mercilessly for the story in *Cars* magazine. He shouted, yelled, and screamed about the points we had made in the article. And that photo! He couldn't get over the photo.

He screamed about our temerity in publishing a photo of their car that had broken while in our care, which he thought was totally unfair. He accused us of abusing the car, which had caused it to break. He said he had never in all his day seen such warped and unbalanced journalism as we had displayed in that article, and that we should be ashamed to call ourselves journalists. This was all screamed into the phone, and he went on like that for several more minutes.

He concluded with: "Oldham, you and all the other people from that rag you call a magazine are immediately and irrevocably banned from attending all American Motors press events. Forever!" With that, he slammed the phone down in my ear.

I put the phone down, stunned. I looked up at Marty and Fred and Al. We were all stunned. Then almost simultaneously, we broke into uncontrollable laughter. The hilarity of it was unbelievable.

Here was the chairman, president, and CEO of a car company, already on its last legs, already fighting for its life, posting loss upon loss upon loss. Yet, this big wheel, the guy running the whole show over there in Kenosha, had nothing better to do than to

Little problems like trim pieces that weren't properly attached took a back seat to bigger problems, like having the back wheel sheer off from the axle in traffic.

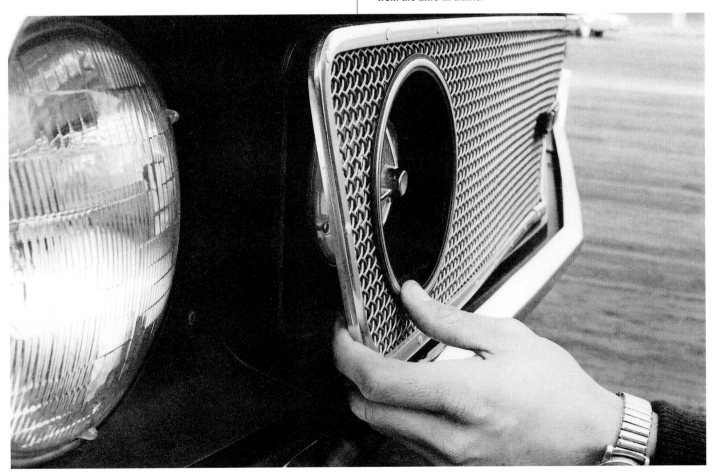

Oldham personally liked the car, even though the magazine gave it a negative (but fair) review.

call a low-life automotive journalist personally, *personally*, mind you, and berate him for seven or eight minutes about an article that he didn't like.

No wonder American Motors failed.

I've thought about that phone call on and off for the past 41 years. Was Gerald C. Meyes right? Were we unfair to this car?

First of all, the boss, Marty Schorr, had a very strict tell-it-like-it-is policy in his magazines, and we all adhered to it. Our editorial mission was to serve the readers. As such, we didn't pussyfoot around if something wasn't up to snuff on a test car. We reported it to readers. The car companies didn't always like that, but it was tough shit. Readers who paid for the magazine came first. So we got calls. Public relations guys called us all the time. But we had never before gotten a call from a president-chairman-CEO.

So, had we been unfair?

Actually, I liked American Motors and its products. We all did at *Cars*. In fact, a few years before, we had run a yearlong series of articles on a Javelin project car that was very popular with readers.

And before the wheel-ripping-off incident and the other quality control issues we had to deal with, I liked driving the '71 Javelin/AMX.

For the '71 model year, AMC discontinued the two-seater AMX because of faltering sales and made

"AMX" a top-of-the-line performance option on the Javelin four-seater pony car. Along with dramatically new—and hairy—styling, the '71 Javelin/AMX made a hard-ass statement on the street, and the new 401 V-8 backed up the looks.

Pumping 330 horsepower at 5,000 rpm and 430 lb-ft of torque at 3,400 rpm through a single Carter four-barrel carb, the car could run well enough not to be embarrassed on the street. Backing the 401 in our test car was a four-speed manual transmission with Hurst linkage and a stiff 3.91 rear axle gear. Our silver-with-black-trim test car also had some optional stuff—scattershield, console, front and rear spoiler, E60-15 Goodyear Polyglas GT tires on styled wheels, and other comfort and convenience options.

I was in charge of track testing this car, so on a Saturday in late May 1971, I drove out to Raceway Park in Englishtown, New Jersey, to run some numbers.

On the first run, I knew it was going to be a tough day. With the tires pumped to factory specs (28 psi all around), I staged, revved to 3,000 rpm and dumped the clutch. The result was so much wheel hop, I thought the entire rear axle housing was going to rip out of the car. Naturally, I let off. The Goodyears provided too much traction for the leaf-spring rear

The Javelin AMX could barely break into the 14-second bracket, but it wasn't because of an underachieving engine; rather, it was because the poorly designed suspension led to so much wheel hop under acceleration that the car couldn't hook up.

suspension to deal with. I pumped the rear tires to 60 psi, thinking I would cut down on the tire's footprint, thereby getting some wheelspin.

No. Still just wheel hop. My notes from that day indicate that we spent about two hours just trying different ways to get off the line—more tire pressure, less tire pressure, more revs, less revs, different drivers, whatever. Finally, I gave up and just rolled out the first few feet, then nailed it.

By the way, before you accuse me of abusing the car, thereby causing the wheel assembly to break off later, as Gerald C. Meyers did, know this. We did the same thing with every test car we ever ran at the track. You've got to make test launches to see what works. Sometimes dozens of them. It's the only way to fairly assess what a car can do in the quarter mile and give it its best shot.

In all my testing experience using these techniques, no other car ever sheared off a wheel-tire-brake drum. OK?

The best my test Javelin/AMX car could do at Raceway Park was a 14.60 elapsed time with a trap speed of 98 mph, which was respectable

for 1971 but certainly not amongst the top rung of muscle cars.

The car fared better on Raceway Park's handling loop, its stiff suspension keeping it flat as it tracked through corners, with the big Goodyears finally succumbing to terminal oversteer at the limit.

But this muscle car test wasn't about acceleration or handling. It was about quality control. A crumbling corporation couldn't keep control of its own assembly lines. As such, this test car had decal stripes peeling off, loose knobs on the dash that dropped off in my hands, loose carpeting that pulled up, a front grille that was barely attached to the car, and then the final indignity, the errant wheel assembly. This last defect could actually have been fatal had it occurred during our high speed track testing or while cruising on a highway.

I never got a chance to ask Gerald C. Meyers about that call because we were all banned from all further American Motors press events and from their proving grounds and were never again invited to any American Motors press conferences.

The car handled well enough, despite the stuttering rear axle. If the car had been developed a bit better and screwed together a lot better, it might have been a winner.

Muscle Car "Enhancers"

4

David Newhardt

Whether it's automobiles, fine food, or sex, nothing sells like excess. Detroit used the last to sell the first. Starting with the GTO, the factories offered power in excess, though handling and braking abilities were in shorter supply. But sheer, straight-line acceleration was the yardstick used to measure the quality of an automobile at the time. The door trim fell off the third day you owned the car? Big deal—it still smoked the tires in every gear! The NHRA was firing on all cylinders, and sanctioned drag racing was growing at a phenomenal rate. Car magazines, extolled thrust, and what better way to show off than to trounce your buddy on a Saturday afternoon at a drag strip? Quarter-mile battlefields sprang up faster than you could grab second gear.

Amid all of this factory-supported mayhem, there was a group of enthusiasts who felt that the big-horsepower engines weren't enough. If they couldn't get the excess they craved at their local dealer, maybe there was a way to inject some beans beneath the hood through the factories back doors. The average muscle car owner didn't have the juice with the car companies to shake loose some of the massive motors produced for "special applications" (code for racing, which, strictly speaking, was banned by all U.S. automakers), but a handful of dealers figured out how to game the system to get ultimate performance. To offer cars in race-ready, turn-key form, they either super-tuned the factory-supplied engines or just yanked out the stock engine and installed small thermonuclear devices. Although these "tuner" dealers, fabled men like Yenko, Tasca, and Mr. Norm, produced vehicles in miniscule numbers; their influence reached from shade-tree mechanic to manufacturer boardroom. Today the cars they produced are some of the most valuable muscle cars ever built.

The extreme performance cars built by Yenko Chevrolet are among the most coveted of all muscle cars.

Royal
Pontiac

It Started as an Experiment

It was 1959, and within the labyrinth of General Motors, Pontiac, led by division general manager Semon E. "Bunkie" Knudsen, was a division in ascent. While the spotlight was on the traditional crosstown rivalry between Ford and Chevrolet, Pontiac was making serious market inroads with its performance cars. Knudsen was a performance enthusiast who wanted Pontiac to step away from its stodgy, granny-mobile image.

When he took over Pontiac in 1956, Knudsen immediately tasked the division with creating products that would shake up the image problem. A bold first step was the 1957 Bonneville, a fuel-injected convertible that sold for the staggering sum of $5,700! Next step was to raid Oldsmobile for a sharp engineer named Elliot M. "Pete" Estes. He followed that by signing up another engineer, a young fellow who was looking for work following the collapse of Studebaker-Packard, John Zachary DeLorean.

For model year 1959, a new breed of Pontiacs was going to be unleashed, incorporating a new design

The Royal Bobcats weren't exactly factory muscle cars, but they were factory-sanctioned.

Royal Bobcats provided a little bling along with their bang.

and a clever ad campaign, centered on the new term "Wide-Track." This phrase was more than simple ad-speak; it described the result of moving the wheels as far out toward the corners of the car as possible, a change made after Knudsen had seen a styling buck of a full-sized Pontiac, which he thought "looked like a football player in ballet slippers." He thought that the tires disappeared under the car.

One of the individuals charged with making the Wide-Track campaign work was Jim Wangers, a young assistant account executive at Pontiac's advertising agency, MacManus, John & Adams. Wangers was a car guy to the marrow and had spent time working at Chevrolet and Chrysler to help shape their performance images. Wangers was well placed at Pontiac.

Knudsen had decreed that a full-court press in the racing world was the best way to get Pontiac's name in front of the public, and in that direction, the Super Duty Group was created to get factory-developed high-performance parts into the right hands. The problem was that most Pontiac dealers knew

more about coddling Grandma's hemorrhoids than they did about drag racing.

Wangers, on the other hand, knew more than most about performance cars and drag racing. He saw Knudsen's edict as an opportunity to connect with the

Not all Royal Bobcats had Tri-Power carburetion. Pontiac's Super Duty catalog had some more practical four-barrel options too.

leading edge of the baby-boomer generation. If boomers could get excited about Pontiac while in their late teens and early twenties, they would carry that excitement with them for life. Wangers presented a proposal to Knudsen and Pontiac sales manager Frank Bridge that would connect dealers with the factory at seminars at the zone offices. These seminars would give interested dealers a chance to learn about and sell performance vehicles, services, and parts. While Knudsen loved the idea, Bridge, who was firmly in the coddling-granny's-hemorrhoids camp, was less than enthralled. Knudsen didn't give Wangers the go-ahead to implement a full-scale program, but he let the young ad man use a single dealership as a test bed. Wangers chose Royal Pontiac in the Detroit suburb of Royal Oak, close to the Pontiac factory. There

The earliest Royal Bobcats weren't quite as flamboyant as later versions.

he spoke with Asa "Ace" Wilson Jr., the son of the part-owner of a successful dairy business, Ira Wilson Dairy. He wasn't the least bit interested in milk and cheese. He was a lover of wine, women, and cars. When his father, Asa Sr., saw that Ace Jr. lacked the self-starting gene, he bought a small Pontiac dealership in Royal Oak and installed his son there to run it.

Wangers walked into the showroom in September 1959 with a proposal. As Ace Jr. listened, he grew excited. He genuinely loved cars and was open to try something new. That day, he signed up for this experiment.

One of the first steps taken at Royal Pontiac was to groom a salesperson in performance. Fortunately, Dick Jesse was a showroom salesman who loved

performance. He got what Wangers had in mind, and soon, customers that came in looking for a thrilling ride were directed to Jesse.

Royal Pontiac dipped a toe into drag racing with encouraging results. Wangers, evidently with time on his hands, shared driving duties behind the wheel of Royal-sponsored Catalinas. Wangers won the NHRA Top Stock Eliminator class at the 1960 Nationals with a run of 14.15 seconds at 100.44 mph.

Business flowed into the dealership, and another leg of the performance stool that Wangers had suggested started to take off. Word on the street got out that cars from Royal Pontiac were tough to beat, and

Even though they were stout performance cars, the early Royal Bobcats were still based on full-sized models like the Catalina and Grand Prix.

the secret was the tune-up service that the dealership offered. Modifications included changing camshaft timing, ignition, spark-plug gap, carburetor jetting, thermostat, and even thinner head gaskets. The result was crisper response and a willingness of the engine to live in the upper range of the tachometer. All of these goodies made up what was called the Royal Bobcat treatment.

All models of Pontiacs could be fitted with the potent Bobcat package, from Catalinas to Grand Prix. But when the GTO debuted in 1964, *Hot Rod* magazine tested a zone manager's wife's example, and the tribe of scribblers was underwhelmed. Wangers was

furious, and he confronted John DeLorean, who was now running Pontiac. The upshot was that Wangers would equip a pair of media test vehicles with every Pontiac performance part he could lay his hands on. For the GTO intended for media drag strip testing, Wangers had Royal Pontiac slip a HO 421 engine from a Bonneville into the GTO. Then the engine was given the Bobcat treatment. Somehow, Wangers forgot to tell the journalists that this wasn't a purely stock GTO. But the write-up in *Car and Driver* magazine made the subterfuge worthwhile. The buff book raved, and the GTO legend was born.

As the 1960s rolled on, Royal Pontiac remained busy, providing Pontiac performance across the country thanks to a thriving mail-order business.

Though a four-barrel would probably be more efficient (and faster) on a 389 than three two-barrels, a Royal Bobcat just doesn't look right without Tri-Power.

The inside of the first Royal Bobcats was all business. The floor-shifted four-speed let people
know the owner was interested in more than just picking up the kids after school.

The new-for-1964 gave Royal the perfect platform for its Bobcat package.

And on-site, Royal's mechanics kept busy. Pontiac had a surplus of 428 HO engines, and Royal would just go up the road to the factory and bring the big engines back to the dealership as needed. For $650, Royal would trade out the stock 400 engine in a GTO car and replace it with a Bobcatted 428. This was, understandably, popular with the public and the press.

With John DeLorean moving to lead Chevrolet in 1969, performance at Pontiac was at risk. In 1970, Royal Pontiac was sold to an out-of-state Chevrolet dealer. That deal didn't last long, and soon Jim Fresard bought the dealership. Fresard left the facility in 2008 for new digs.

Ace Wilson Jr. died on March 18, 1984, and he left behind an impressive legacy in the performance world. His dealership was the first true performance dealer, selling street cars and not race cars. Ace Wilson Jr. and Jim Wangers made money selling speed. While others would try to emulate the operation, there was only one Royal Pontiac.

This emblem meant performance in the 1960s.

128

Nickey
Chevrolet

Windy City Performance

The story begins during the Great Depression, when Chicago, like the rest of the country, was struggling. A local dealership, located on the northwest side of the city, owned by Mr. Nickey, was purchased during the 1930s by two brothers, Edward "E. J." Stephani, and his younger sibling, John, also called Jack. The brothers divided the workload, with Jack running the showroom and Ed the back of the store.

In 1957, while on vacation in Florida, Jack noticed a local business that had inserted a backward letter in its name. He remembered it as attention-getting, and when he returned to Chicago, he contacted a sign company to paint "Nickey" on one of the side walls of the dealership with the *k* reversed.

A Camaro with a stock 396 was no slouch; with a 427, it was a rocket ship.

It didn't take clever dealerships long to figure out that swapping the 396-cubic-inch engine in a Camaro SS396 was a simple bolt-in process.

Nickey Chevrolet began selling converted 427 Camaros almost as soon as Chevrolet began building Camaros.

Immediately, people were coming into the dealership to tell the owners that their sign was wrong. The foot traffic turned into sales.

In the late 1950s, Nickey Chevrolet got into racing, and it sponsored the famous 1958 *Purple People Eater* Corvette. At the end of the '58 season, the vivid race car had won the B/Production Championship.

Though the remainder of the 1950s and well into the 1960s, Nickey Chevrolet sponsored a wide range of race cars, from NASCAR to sports cars. Actor Dan Blocker of the TV show *Bonanza* owned a Genie Mk X USRRC car called the *Vinegaroon*. Nickey Chevrolet became the vehicle's sponsor, and in return, Blocker did commercials for the dealership.

In 1965, Nickey vice president Don Selieg approached parts manager Don Swiatek and asked if he thought a performance shop would work. Swiatek said that he felt it would, so Selieg told him that he had 30 days to make it work or he'd be out a job. The body shop was converted to a speed shop, and word quickly spread that the crew at Nickey could handle any performance task. A customer looking for a four-wheel rocket would settle on a car with the regular sales staff, and then the "up" would be handed to Swiatek, who would work with the customer to have the car outfitted with a wide range of performance options.

Nickey Chevrolet had another way to get customers into the showroom: fly them in! Nickey would pay for a one-way ticket from anywhere in the United

While Nickey didn't embellish its Camaros with as much ornamentation as Yenko and Baldwin-Motion, it did include a few tasteful emblems.

The driver probably didn't need the badge below the shifter to let him know what lurked under the hood; his right foot probably already told him.

States for a customer who wanted a performance car unlike any in his or her hometown.

In Southern California, a fellow named Bill Thomas, who had built the brutally fast Cheetah race car, was available for work. Negotiations ensued, and toward the end of 1966, Thomas ended up becoming Nickey's West Coast presence. Thomas, who was the force behind the potent 377-cubic-inch monster in the Cheetah, came on board with Nickey.

Part of the deal was to sponsor famed drag racer Dick Harrell. A skilled mechanic blessed with legendary reflexes, Harrell made a huge impact on the genesis of the funny car. Harrell did so well driving in the first half of 1966 in the Nickey car that Nickey hired him full-time to pilot a Thomas-built Chevy II drag car.

Meanwhile, Chevrolet introduced its response to Ford's Mustang, the Camaro, in the autumn of 1966. In Southern California, Dana Chevrolet had installed a 427-cubic-inch engine from a 1966 Corvette into the Camaro with frightening results. Word quickly got out that the engine compartment of the Camaro, designed to accommodate the externally identical 396, swallowed the bigger engine with ease. At Nickey, Don Swiatek wasted no time slipping a 427/435-horsepower engine in the little four-seater, and Nickey was selling super cars. Before you could say "four-speed," Swiatek had his four master mechanics handling engine swaps for a line of customers. Most of the Rat engine installations in 1967 Camaros were done at Thomas' Anaheim, California, shop. This wasn't a cheap vehicle: a Stage III 427 Nickey/Thomas Camaro cost $5,922, $1,500 more than a new Corvette. Of course, 550 horsepower helped justify the price.

Nickey Chevrolet had a thriving mail-order parts department as well. Every Chevy enthusiast looked forward to their letter carrier delivering the Nickey Chevrolet Speed Parts catalog, a veritable dream list

While this might look like an ordinary 1967 Camaro, it didn't act like one.

Nickey didn't use custom seat covers like those used on the Yenko Super Cars.

of go-fast goodies. If a part was designed for performance and Chevrolet made it, you could have it sent to your house. Even the $1 cost of the catalog was refunded with the first order! The mail-order business was good for the bottom line; in the mid-1960s, the Nickey Speed Shop was pulling in more than $60,000 a month. In the basement of the dealership was a cinder-block room called the Vault. Inside were the high-dollar crate engines, long- and short-blocks, waiting to be installed. One owner of a 1969 ZL-1 Camaro recalls driving his pickup truck to Nickey, walking down into the Vault, choosing three new ZL-1 engines, and then loading them into his truck.

As the 1960s were drawing to a close, clouds were starting to gather above Nickey Chevrolet. A number of incidents in 1967 set the stage for trouble, including tax problems, an employee theft ring, financing issues, and the Stephanis' efforts to keep the unions at bay.

By 1973, General Motors was knocking on the door, as Nickey was "out of trust," meaning they were selling cars but not paying GM. In response, Nickey closed the doors in December 1973. In its day, Nickey Chevrolet had a higher profile than any other performance dealer. With its successful involvement in a wide range of motorsports, few people weren't aware of the backward k. Nickey helped spread the gospel of performance from coast to coast.

The reversed *k* in the Nickey logo was meant to attract attention. It did.

Dana Chevrolet

Eighteen Months of Fun

The roots for Dana Chevrolet grew within one man at Ford, more specifically at Shelby American: Peyton Cramer. Cramer worked for Ford in the early 1960s in the Ford Division controller's office, under Ray Geddes in special vehicle operations. He was tapped by Geddes to go to Los Angeles to help run Carroll Shelby's operation.

Cramer straightened up the Shelby organization and turned it into a profitable enterprise. He worked as general manager for two years until mid-1965. In 1966, with the bulk of Shelby operations moving under the control of Ford in Dearborn, he left Shelby and approached Ford about becoming an automobile dealer. Ford said that he had no retail experience. He knew famed racer Dick Guldstrand, who had ties to Chevrolet, and Guldstrand suggested that Cramer talk to the bowtie crowd.

Peyton found a dealership that had shuttered and through his wife met Paul Dombroski. Dombroski owned a Mercedes-Jeep dealership. Cramer and Dombroski teamed up and acquired the dealership, and they called it Dana Chevrolet after the side street next to the facility. It was quickly decided that Dombroski would handle the dealership located at 8730 Long Beach Boulevard while Cramer would be in charge of racing activities down the street at 9735 Long Beach Boulevard.

The racing center was called Dana Hi-Performance Center, and it was a full-service dealership, as long as buyers wanted Corvettes and Camaros. It had a showroom, parts, and service departments, everything a normal dealership had. To staff it, Cramer approached the very same mechanics who had worked at Shelby's shop. As a result, he was able to get a first-class racing effort up and running in a matter of weeks.

Cramer recalls getting the facility converted into a race shop. "We tore the floor out of the shop and then poured another one so that it would be perfectly level so that when we set the race cars up, everything was level. It was the same thing we did at Shelby in the hangers."

To run the Center, Cramer contacted Dick Guldstrand, who found himself at loose ends when, as Guldstrand recalls, "Mr. Penske decided to let me go. Well, he was mad at me when I crashed his car and got hurt really bad. He wasn't going to pay me until he found out I was going to live." Guldstrand was good friends with Zora Arkus-Duntov and Ed Cole, so he "brought a lot to the party."

Cramer says, "He acted as the go-between with General Motors, and he did all the engineering."

As soon as the Center was open, Cramer and Guldstrand put together a plan to campaign a Corvette race car. Sunray Oil from Oklahoma was the primary sponsor, and the 1967 Corvette coupe was fitted with an L88 427-cubic-inch engine, race prepared at the Dana Hi-Performance Center.

Off to the 24 Hours of Le Mans the car went, and it ran well until the 13th hour, when a wristpin failed. Chevrolet had insisted that the internal components of the engine remain untouched, and it was a factory part that had been identified as needing replacement before the race that let go.

Dana Chevrolet backed the 1967 Can-Am entry driven by Peter Revson and Bob Bondurant. After a severe crash, Bondurant was replaced by Lothar Motschenbacher behind the wheel of the McLaren. The dealership existed to allow Cramer to go racing.

Word got out in Los Angeles that the Dana Hi-Performance Center could supply buyers with scary-fast cars and superb tune-up work. When Peyton Cramer had worked at Shelby, he had observed that transplanting an engine was a saleable idea, so when he opened his own performance center, he suggested his crew that a bit of mechanical switcheroo might be possible. When the Camaro debuted in 1967, it was not offered with a big-block engine until some months later. Don McCain, who followed Cramer from Shelby, was a drag racer, mechanic, and sales manager. He said that he took a look at the new Camaro and thought, "Oh, lookie here. I called the parts center up in Oakland to find out what a 427 Corvette engine costs. They said $900. I said, 'You better send me one.' We dropped that puppy in, and we're selling Dana Camaros for $3,995."

Cramer recalls being behind the wheel of one of his 427 Camaros. "It was really hairy. It wasn't as hairy as a 427 Cobra, because of the weight, but it was probably as close as you could come to driving a 427 Cobra. The power to weight ratio . . . you know, those cars weren't that heavy. It got your attention."

In the spring of 1968, Cramer remembers, "I had a falling out with Dombroski, and Chevrolet was getting out of racing: they sort of pulled the plug." Cramer decided to sell off his interest in Dana to Dombroski, as well as all of his racing equipment, including cars and parts, to Carroll Shelby. Ironically, some of Shelby's former employees followed the cars, becoming Shelby employees again. The end was at hand.

Dombroski tried to run Dana by himself, but that quickly fell apart, and the dealership was sold to Cormier Chevrolet. When Dombroski left the facilities, he threw away all of the records, including production information on all of the high-performance vehicles. Hence, today it's very difficult to authenticate a genuine Dana performance car.

Eighteen months doesn't seem like a long period of time, but it was long enough to make a strong mark on the performance world. Dana Chevrolet was the result of the right people, with the right experience, being in the right place at the right time.

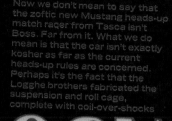

Now we don't mean to say that the zoftic new Mustang heads-up match racer from Tasca isn't Boss. Far from it. What we do mean is that the car isn't exactly kosher as far as the current heads-up rules are concerned. Perhaps it's the fact that the Logghe brothers fabricated the suspension and roll cage, complete with coil-over-shocks

BOGUS BOSS

all around. Or the fact that Al Bergler did the aluminum floor and trunk. Or how about the fiberglass hood, doors, decklid and splash pans? Then there's always that super thin glass, and what appears to be a plexiglass windshield. Needless to say, none of the above attributes are in keeping with the current heads-up racing ground rules. Likewise, injectors are a deviation from the carburetor rule, and no matter how hard we tried, we couldn't get our magnet to grab hold of that cylinder block. Could it be that it's one of those aluminum 494-inchers, rather than a cast iron 429?

Ektachromes by Don Green

Tasca Ford

Cars for the Taker, not the Maker

Hollywood couldn't make this stuff up. Boy joins company, works his way up, company owner skims the money, blows it on the ponies. Boy gets fed up, quits, and strikes out on his own, cue massive success. Add race cars and captains of industry, mix in some family, more success. The end. Funny thing is, it's the truth. Welcome to Tasca Ford.

Bob Tasca Sr. was born in 1928, and as he turned 16, he was busy building his own cars, hopping up engines, and doing body work. In 1948, he went to work for Harry Sandager at his car lot in Cranston,

Rhode Island, essentially as a gofer. It didn't take long for Tasca to get fed up with menial tasks and make Sandager a proposal.

Tasca remembers, "He had 70 used cars that were really doing nothing but sitting there because they needed work. I said, 'I'd like to offer you a proposition: I'll fix those cars; you pay for the parts, I'll pay for the labor. It won't cost you a dime to work on 'em. We'll split the profits, 75 percent for you, 25 percent for me.' Sandager thought about it for a while and said, 'Do it.' Well, I made $26,000 for my

Bob Tasca III showed Ford how to build a proper Mustang muscle car.

Though it might have had an old-tech 428 lump of an engine, the Tasca Mustang showed Ford's Boss 429 who was really the boss.

share. When Mr. Sandager saw this, he said that I should take over reconditioning." That led to a series of promotions, culminating with a position as general manager.

But there was a problem. Enjoying the good life was not unusual for Harry Sandager. He'd been a member of the State House of Representatives, and then he got elected to Congress from 1939 to 1941. As Tasca notes, "I couldn't stand him because he took all the money we made to the racetrack. If there was five grand in the bank, he'd take four grand and go to the racetrack. I used to buy used cars. I couldn't pay for them. I'd have to wait until I'd sold it, then go back and pay the other dealer."

Tasca had enough and left Sandager to open his own dealership in 1953 in Bristol, Rhode Island, at an establishment that had sold just 30 cars a year. Tasca came in and sold 126 units in the first two months. But what he really wanted was to be a Ford dealer. He contacted Dearborn and ended up taking over a Bristol Ford dealership that had moved a whopping 31 cars a year for the prior three years. When Tasca

took over, the numbers climbed to 135 cars a year for the first two years. That got Ford's attention.

However, things have a way of turning out slightly different than planned, and the catalyst for change was in the form of a Category 3 storm named Hurricane Carol in August 1954. The massive hurricane wiped out Tasca's dealership. Ford offered him a dealership closer to his home market, near East Providence, Rhode Island. Tasca agreed to step into the dealership on a trial basis, and by the end of September 1954, he'd sold 144 cars. More attention from Dearborn.

Tasca quickly became one of the biggest-selling Ford dealerships in the country, and Ford was curious as to how he how he sold so many vehicles. When asked for his secret by Ford, Tasca showed the company how he put customers first and foremost. Tasca got to know Henry Ford II, and in 1963, "The Deuce" offered Tasca $3 million to work for Ford and teach its employees how to sell. Bob Tasca told Henry that he'd go anywhere for the company, do anything

for the company, but he wouldn't take a dime. When Ford asked him why he wouldn't take any money, Tasca replied, "Just build the right cars. I'll sell plenty of them and make money." Eventually, Tasca would train over 165,000 Ford employees on the "right" way to do business.

In the early 1960s, Chevrolet was a growing powerhouse with a massive share of the market. Or,

as Tasca put it, "Chevy was kicking the hell out of us. So I said to Henry Ford II in 1962, 'I need your help. I want to build a performance car to compete with Chevrolet, because they're taking all the business.' Ford said 'Do it.' I told Henry that the people who worked for him didn't understand the car business.

They built a car to suit the maker; I sold a car that suited the taker."

Tasca had started drag racing a 406-cubic-inch Galaxie 500 in 1962. But Tasca recalls, "It was not as successful as I wanted because it was too much car. Then I went to a Fairlane, and that went better; as it evolved, it just cleaned house. Driver Bill Lawton was Tasca's hired gun behind the wheel until 1971.

With the knowledge gleaned from the drag program, Tasca approached Ford. As he saw it, Ford was taking the wrong approach to selling performance. "What we needed was a street machine. Ford was in NASCAR building race cars. I don't sell race cars, I sell street cars. So I said to Henry, 'You've been spending millions in NASCAR. I don't know how many cars that's sold for you, but I do know this. If you build a street performance car, you'll sell a lot of them.' At the peak, I sold over 100 a month."

Chevrolet debuted the Camaro in 1967, and from the beginning, it could be equipped with the potent 396-cubic-inch big-block engine. All Ford had in the competing Mustang was a 390-cubic-inch mill that, frankly, just didn't get the job done. Tasca had seen Mustang sales start to fall off as the impressive Camaro started pulling enthusiasts into Chevrolet showrooms. This wouldn't do in East Providence. The answer came in the form of a damaged engine.

The engine work done at Tasca led to the creation of the Cobra Jet and Super Cobra Jet engines.

One of his employees had over-revved the engine in a 390-equipped Mustang, so Tasca's high-performance manager Dean Gregson had his crew replace the 390 FE block with a 428-cubic-inch Police Interceptor block. On top of the big piece of iron went a pair of 427 low-riser heads and a 735 cfm Holley carburetor. Inside the block was a 390 GTA hydraulic camshaft. The resulting engine, called the KR8, would make Ford history.

Except Ford didn't take the engine seriously at first. At least not until the power of the press came onto the scene in the form of *Hot Rod* magazine. Its technical editor, Eric Dahlquist, heard that Tasca had put together some kind of performance engine. While on a family vacation, he pulled into Tasca Ford to check out the new engine. He took his impressions back to Los Angeles, where in the next issue of the magazine, he put a "ballot" in, asking readers if they would like to see Ford build the engine. The overwhelming results were sent to Henry Ford II.

In the meantime, Tasca used his influence with The Deuce to show the corporation what his shop had created. The engineering department was impressed with what they saw, and when the flood of mail from *Hot Rod* readers arrived on Ford's desk, the die was cast. Ford engineering was put to work creating a production version of Tasca's engine. Ford released the new powerplant, dubbed the Cobra Jet, in mid-1968 in a run of 50 Mustangs with consecutive VINs. Ford offered it in regular-production 1969 Mustangs, Cougars, and midsized Fords and Mercurys. The engine did wonders for Ford's street-performance credibility.

For a dealer to be taken seriously in the performance market in the 1960s, there had to have more on the table than just fast cars for sale. Service and parts played a huge role in expanding a dealership's influence in enthusiast circles. Modifing customers'

cars and supplying them with over-the-counter parts to install themselves was big business in the late 1960s; Tasca was selling over $100,000 a month in performance parts alone.

Tasca devised a clever system for selling parts, based on car lengths. Someone would come into the dealership, and Tasca would ask, "How bad did you get beaten last weekend?" The car owner might say two car lengths. Tasca would reply, "This package will give you four car lengths."

Tasca was always building performance cars at the dealership and then testing them at a local drag strip. He knew what combination of parts would work and by how much. He could deliver consistent car lengths, for a price. If the car didn't deliver as promised, Tasca's policy was that the customer got the package for free. In all his years in the performance field, he never gave a package away.

As the 1970s dawned, a combination of factors, especially rising insurance rates and the need for auto manufacturers to build vehicles that could meet the increasingly stringent emission regulations, would shove the performance cars off the showroom floor. Tasca was reluctant to compete on the drag strip on a vehicle that wasn't powered by gasoline. He felt that a production-car dealership should compete with street-type cars, not vehicles fueled by alcohol or nitro. Tasca said that he felt, "If I can't sell it on Monday, I don't want to race it on Sunday. I'm not in the business to win races; I'm in the business to sell cars."

Performance continues to motivate Tasca Ford. Bob Tasca III actively campaigns a Mustang Funny Car. In 2007, Shelby and Tasca announced a collaboration in which Tasca would become the East Coast headquarters for Shelby American, including vehicle modification. It's clear that horsepower helped propel Tasca to the front ranks of the performance field, and they have no intention of pulling back.

Baldwin-
Motion

Bringing a Gun to a Knife Fight

You never know where the performance gene will show itself. Here's a kid from Brooklyn, Joel Rosen, whose parents didn't have a car until he was 16. When he took his first driving test, he crashed into a telephone pole and bent the front axle. But when the performance bug bit him, Rosen started racing. He wiped out his 1958 Fuelie Corvette in a hill climb race, so he got a '62 Fuelie. When the 1963 Corvette hit the street, Rosen was in love. Buying a fuel-injected coupe, he flogged it at drag strips throughout the area and used it to commute to the Sunaco

gas station where he was a junior partner. In 1963, he convinced his partner that the station needed a Clayton chassis dynamometer and an oscilloscope. There were only a couple of dynamometers in the entire Northeast, and using it in conjunction with a Sun Diagnosis oscilloscope allowed Rosen to fine-tune an engine under load. It was this same year that a new sign went up in front of the station, "Motion Performance."

Joel was an early convert to electronic ignition systems, and he used a capacitive discharge system

Joel Rosen knew that a muscle car had to look fast as well as be fast. The cars built by Baldwin-Motion were both.

Buyers could get their Baldwin-Motion cars tuned virtually any way they wanted them. More often than not, those cars were the fastest around.

called the Motion EI 5 CD. He borrowed the name for his own business. The editor of *Cars* magazine, Martyn Schorr, wrote an article about a Corvette that Rosen had built, and the two men hit it off. Schorr would figure prominently in the future of Motion Performance and the creation of Baldwin-Motion.

Word quickly got out that Rosen knew how to make a car really run, and business was good. But the neighborhood wasn't, and when, as Rosen puts it, "they started shooting back instead of talking back," he was out of there. It was 1966, and he pulled stakes and headed out to Long Island's Sunrise Highway in Baldwin, New York.

After six months in the new location, his partner didn't want to be involved anymore, so Rosen bought him out. Joel worked on customer's cars, using nearby Baldwin Chevrolet as a source of factory parts, and he

The cockpit of a Motion-Performance Camaro was not a place for the timid.

became friends with the dealership's parts manager, John Mahler. Mahler helped Rosen put together a presentation for a program that Rosen and Schorr had been planning. Joel proposed an arrangement with Baldwin Chevrolet's owner that would allow customers to buy a new car at the dealership, then have it sent down the street to Motion Performance, where it would be outfitted with the exact speed equipment the buyer wanted, while still being a new car with a warranty.

Strictly a mom-and-pop dealership, Baldwin Chevrolet was run by Ed Simonin. Baldwin Chevy was the kind of dealership that catered to the sale of mainstream vehicles such as the Impala and Chevelle, but Rosen convinced them that if they would supply the cars, he would then set them up for performance, and Baldwin Chevrolet would become famous. That's pretty much what happened.

With the introduction of the Camaro in 1967, Joel Rosen and Marty Schorr were ready to put Rosen's idea into action. Baldwin gave Rosen a couple of

L88. 427. Really, what more do you need to know?

vehicles to build as prototypes and agreed to pick up the advertising bills. Rosen was given anything he needed: engines, parts, anything. The prototype car Joel assembled was a '67 Camaro equipped with a 427-cubic-inch engine.

He told the folks at Baldwin, "We couldn't do this [the street car program] unless we built a race car, because if you don't race, people aren't going to believe the cars are fast. . . . I thought we needed a drag vehicle." So Rosen built his drag car, filling the engine compartment with one of the first L88 427-cubic-inch engines released through the GM parts network.

Success came quickly on the drag strip, and it spilled over to the sale of streetable cars. The crew at Motion Performance numbered about 20, and they weren't hurting for work. Schorr kept

the Baldwin-Motion name front and center in enthusiast magazines, and the publicity and advertising paid off.

Except for the demo cars that Joel Rosen kept handy, virtually every car Baldwin-Motion built was a bespoke vehicle. Customers with money burning holes in their pockets had three ways to put a Baldwin-Motion ground-pounder in the garage. The first was mail order. Motion Performance mailed hundreds of catalogs to American military forces fighting in the Vietnam War. Often, servicemen would order and pay for a vehicle while overseas, then upon their return to the States, swing by Baldwin, New York, to pick up the car.

Another path to ownership was to actually go to Motion Performance and talk with Joel Rosen. There were always a couple of Motion cars on the premises, and any wavering by a potential customer was banished when Rosen would take them for a test drive. He would write up the order depending on the wants and needs of the customer and then take the order to Baldwin Chevrolet.

The third way was to walk into Baldwin Chevrolet and ask to speak with someone about a Baldwin-Motion car. When the Baldwin-Motion partnership was in its infancy, some of the sales staff were afraid of losing a commission, so they would steer customers toward a 396/375 Camaro rather than sending them down to Motion Performance. Once the owners of Baldwin Chevrolet learned of this, they decreed that anyone looking for a Motion product would be dealing with the dealership owners personally. End of problem.

Being Motion Performance, the line between drag strip and street was blurred with the road versions, especially when customers ordered the top-of-the-line Phase III Package. Rosen put his money where his mouth was when he stated, "We think so much of our Phase III Supercars that we guarantee

Yes, a Camaro with upwards of 500 horsepower can spin the rear tires.

they will turn at least 120 mph in 11.50 seconds or better with an M/P-approved driver on an AHRA- or NHRA-sanctioned drag strip." In all of his years doing business, Rosen never paid out a dime because of failing to fulfill that promise.

Baldwin-Motion cars came in two flavors, SS and Phase III. The SS cars were given upgrades according to the buyer's needs and budget. The Phase III cars, while street legal, were little more than race cars with a license plate frame.

The full range of Chevrolet passenger cars were fair game for the Motion treatment, such as the Camaro, Chevelle, Corvette, Vega, and Nova. The success of Motion Performance allowed Rosen to indulge in the creation of an occasional limited-edition run of cars, such as the Motion GT, Maco Shark, Spyder, and the Manta Ray. These vehicles started life as Corvettes, but Rosen transformed them into wild, powerfully stylistic rolling statements.

Eventually, Baldwin Chevrolet was sold and became Williams Chevrolet, then sold again to become Lyons Chevrolet. That incarnation closed its doors in 1974, forcing Rosen to look to other local Chevy dealerships to supply him with new cars.

Things progressed until 1974, when a *Car Craft* magazine article, "King Kong lives on Long Island," about the 454 Motion Super Vega hit the newsstands. This caught the eye of the Environmental Protection Agency, who took issue with the removal of the stock emission equipment and responded with a fine of $50,000 for each car built. The Feds descended onto Motion Performance with a cease and desist order, effectively shutting down business.

In 1975, Rosen settled with the government. But even that didn't stop the former racer from building high-performance vehicles. The difference from before was that the new cars were labeled "For Export" or "For Off Road Use Only."

In the early 1980s, Rosen built a number of Motion IROC Camaros and Monte Carlos. And at the 2005 SEMA show, Joel Rosen and Mary Schorr unveiled a 1969 Camaro SuperCoupe fitted with a Kinsler-injected aluminum 540-cubic-inch engine, generating in excess of 600 horsepower. With the sophistication of today's on-board computer systems, Rosen is able to extract massive horsepower while maintaining socially responsible emissions.

Grand Spaulding
Dodge

Pentastar Performance

Norm Kraus grew up pumping gas at his father's service station on the northwest corner of West Grand Avenue and North Spaulding Avenue in Chicago, Illinois, a predominantly blue-collar neighborhood. That's how Grand Spaulding Dodge started.

Like so many teenagers following World War II, Kraus was in love with performance. But he didn't want to pump gas and twist wrenches. He sold his father, Harvey, on the idea that having a couple of cars wearing *For Sale* signs on a portion of the station property might bring in a few extra dollars. It was 1948, and Norm, with his brother Lenny, grew skilled in the art of selling used cars under the banner of Grand Spaulding Motors.

Business was so good that in 1951, they bought the lot next door, filled it with cars for sale, strung some lights over them, and moved even more metal. Their father's service station handled needed repairs, and in 1957, the brothers decided to specialize in

from the normal used-car offerings: hot Oldsmobiles, Buicks, and Chryslers, anything that wore a whiff of performance. The brothers approached other dealers, who were having a hard time selling performance cars. The Kraus brothers put tiny, two-line ads in the *Chicago Sun Times* encouraging performance-hungry readers to "Call Mr. Norm." The moniker stuck.

As the 1950s wound to a close, a regional Dodge rep looking to sign up franchisees would stop by the lot periodically and talk to the brothers about becoming a Dodge dealership, but the Kraus brothers were underwhelmed with the look of Dodge vehicles in the early 1960s, and they told the rep that. He assured them that Chrysler had gotten a new designer, and that in the near future, Dodge would have some good-looking vehicles. Finally, they acquiesced, signing up with Dodge in the fall of 1962.

They didn't have a showroom or proper service facilities, but they had an order pad. From the beginning, they stressed performance cars. The entire first order from the factory was Max Wedge cars with thinly disguised racing engines. Kraus figured that he'd get one car now, maybe two later.

more sporting vehicles. This started when an insurance adjuster came into the lot with a 1956 Chevrolet convertible that had seen better days. The brothers placed an ad in the local paper saying: "1956 Chevy convertible, V-8, stick. Call Mr. Norm." The phone rang off the hook.

Norm told Lenny, who was out buying cars to sell on the lot, "That's it, no more regular cars. Buy every car with a V-8 and a stick that you can find." Big engines and manual transmissions stood out

He didn't realize that Max Wedge cars were batch built. Imagine Kraus's surprise when a line of transporters pulled up in a blizzard with the entire order. As the cars rolled off the trucks, sawhorses were set up surrounding them to form a corral to make it look like this kind of collection of high-performance machinery was an everyday occurrence. It didn't take long of the whole batch to find new homes.

In the spring of 1963, the old gas station was torn down and a three-car showroom was built. With Lenny handling the promotion, budgets, sales, and ordering, Norm was the highly visible face of Grand Spaulding Dodge; his smiling visage graced ads for years. Norm and Lenny studied other dealerships, seeing what worked and what didn't, and built what would become the biggest Dodge dealership on Earth.

The brothers started the "Mr. Norm's Sport Club." Buyers of a performance car were automatically enrolled, and benefits included window decals, license plate frames, a monthly newsletter, and a subscription to *Drag News*. Grand Spaulding became a major Mopar Mecca.

In 1963, Grand Spaulding Dodge got into racing. A former customer who had bought one of the Max Wedge cars approached Norm Kraus with a proposal; if Grand Spaulding would supply him with a set of spark plugs and a pair of seat belts, he'd put the dealership's name on the side of his car. Kraus figured what the hell and gave him the parts. That weekend, the car was raced at the Chicago Amphitheater, with the feature being indoor drag racing. The

Grand Spaulding–sponsored car won the race. Come Monday, the phone was ringing off the hook. Grand Spaulding sold three cars that day to people who had seen the race car in action.

A racing team was formed in 1964, made up of two cars, a Max Wedge and a Hemi Ram. By the end of the year, Gary Dyer had been signed up to handle driving chores, and a clever approach was conceived. The dealership made a point to compete in classes that its customer base would not be driving in. That way, the Grand Spaulding entry wouldn't embarrass a customer.

With performance demand ramping up, the Krauses asked Dodge for a car that could compete with the Chevrolet Nova. Dodge sent Grand Spaulding a 1967 Dart with a 273-cubic-inch V-8. Kraus called and asked where the 383 engine was, and he was told that the engine wouldn't fit under the Dart's hood. Kraus told his parts manager to take the small-block out and see what it would take to install the big-block. The next morning, Kraus was told that the car was ready. By moving the motor mounts a little, notching the K-member, and installing a heat shield to protect the steering box, the car was on the road. The resulting potent package was shown to Dodge executives and engineers, who saw a low-cost street bruiser. The factory would release it as the Dart 383 GTS.

Mr. Norm figured that if a 383 fit, what about a 440? It fit, but the exhaust headers had to be run through cut-outs in the inner fender wells, resulting in the GSS 440.

Grand Spaulding fed the need for Mopar performance through the 1960s, becoming the number-one Dodge dealership in the world in 1974. But as the 1970s rolled on, it was clear that the performance market was fading away as tough federal rules regarding emissions dovetailed with rising insurance rates to doom the traditional muscle car. The dealership stepped away from muscle and got into van conversions. When America's youth embraced tricked-out vans, Grand Spaulding benefited from the trend.

Another big source of income was fleet sales to police, government agencies, and rental-car companies. So widespread was Grand Spaulding leasing, it was able to supply the entire Chicago Police Department with its cruisers. Many of these Mr. Norm cars can be seen in the movie *The Blues Brothers*.

Grand Spaulding Dodge closed its doors in 1975, and Norm Kraus retired in 1977, having led the dealership to dizzying heights. Yet Kraus isn't finished with high performance. He's developed a "new" 1968 Dart, now packing a 735-horsepower Hemi. It runs 10-second quarter-mile times. Not a bad run for a kid selling cars at his father's gas station.

Fred Gibb
Chevrolet

Tiny Dealership, Huge Impact

La Harpe, Illinois, is a tiny farming community not far from the Mississippi River that once had a small Chevrolet dealership. Fred Gibb Jr. opened his dealership in 1948, and for many years, he sold a lot of pickups and family sedans. He employed about a dozen people, and he was comfortable. In 1961, he erected a new building and brought on a new employee, Herb Fox.

Before he started at Gibb Chevrolet, Fox was a drag-racing enthusiast. Fred Gibb didn't care for drag racing, thinking that it attracted the wrong kind of crowd. Yet Fox was the dealership's best salesman; in 1965, Fox sold 368 cars out of the small dealership. One day in 1966, Fox was about to head out for another weekend of racing at the local strip in Cahokia, Illinois, when Gibb approached him and asked what he was doing. Fox remembers, "I told him I was going racing. He asked if he could come along. I figured it would probably be my job. I said okay, 'If you want to go, get in.' We came back, and he'd changed his mind about racing."

When Chevrolet debuted the 1967 Camaro, Gibb ordered a Z/28 as a demonstrator. Soon, he asked Fox if he'd like to go in on a race car. Fox said that he didn't want to spend all that money. Gibb replied, "That's okay, I'll just take the demo and make a race car out of it, and you can drive."

But there was a hitch, as Fox remembers. "He wanted to run it

stock, and you can't win running stock. It was May or June, and I'd gone down to St. Louis to see a Cardinals game. Somehow I got lost in East St. Louis. I pulled into a gas station asking directions how to get back across the river; I'd pulled into Dick Harrell's place. He was building 427 Camaros there."

Harrell asked Fox, "What do you do?"

Fox answered, "I sell cars at Fred Gibb Chevrolet. Are these cars for sale?"

"Yes," Harrell said. "I've got a red one and a black one. They have 427s with dual quads."

Fox said that he had to talk to his boss. "When I got back to La Harpe, I told Fred about them, and he said to 'get in the car, we're going to St. Louis.' We went down there and bought both of them." Harrell started working with Gibb, improving their Z/28, and when the season had ended, the Royal Plum Camaro called *Little Hoss* had earned 35 wins in 1967.

Fred Gibb was friends with Vince Piggins, the engineering chief at Chevrolet. Gibb asked Piggins if

Perhaps the ultimate Camaros were the result of a small dealership called Gibb Chevrolet gaming the system to create the fabled ZL-1 cars.

Few people wanted a race car with frills, and the RS languished until it was gussied up with a few additional stripes.

it was possible to order a big engine in a small car. Piggins told Fred about the Central Office Production Order (COPO) system. Gibb was told that they could put L78 396-cubic-inch engines in Chevy II Novas, but the minimum order had to be 50 units. Fred placed the order for a batch of COPO #9738 Chevy II Novas.

By July 15, 1968, all 50 cars had been built and delivered to La Harpe. Fox remembers that Gibb Chevrolet sold all of the COPO Novas at full sticker without a single trade-in. Fred Gibb decided to order another batch of performance cars. Once again, Vince Piggins was approached, and this time the engine would be a 427-cubic-inch mill, but not just any 427; the engine in mind was the new ZL-1. With its aluminum block, head, and intake manifold, the big-block only weighed 500 pounds, about the same as a 327-cubic-inch engine. Built to compete in the Can-Am series, the ZL-1s installed in Camaros were your basic de-tuned racing engine. It developed well over 500 horsepower, with more than 450 lb-ft of torque.

Gibb placed the order for COPO #9560 Camaros and waited. He had been told by Chevrolet that this street-legal race car would cost about $4,900 each. Gibb felt that enough racers would pony up that amount of money to make the order worthwhile. The first two cars arrived at the La Harpe dealership

Most ZL-1 Camaros were plain-Jane racing platforms, except for this one—the only ZL-1 equipped with an RS package.

The aluminum ZL-1 engine was never meant to be a street engine.

on December 31, 1968, in minus-22-degree weather. Surprisingly, neither car would start; a tow truck was used to get them off the trailer.

When the first bill for the cars showed up on his desk, the invoice showed that Gibb owed $7,269 for each car. Fred called Chevrolet and asked about the hefty price increase over the original estimate. Chevy responded with the news that starting in 1969, the word had come down from on high that research and development costs associated with limited-run vehicles would be borne by the customer. In this case, that would be Fred Gibb Chevrolet.

Gibb explained to Chevrolet that the huge price jump was going to make it impossible for him to buy all 50 ZL-1 Camaros. Chevy, in an unprecedented move, agreed to buy back the bulk of the cars. Fox

remembered, "We got 13 sold, but we didn't know what we were going to do with the rest of them. We pulled into Detroit for the drags, and Gibb got called up to the tower. When he came down, I asked him what happened. He said that the general manager thought it [the ZL-1] was the hot deal and wanted one. I told him to come to La Harpe and take them. He came with a semi and took all but one. We had it two years before we ever got rid of it." Eventually, a total of just 69 ZL-1 Camaros were built.

Fred Gibb stepped away from racing at the end of the 1971 season; he saw the writing on the wall, and he knew that street performance was coming to an end. He went back to selling bread-and-butter vehicles.

Gibb sold the dealership in 1984 and retired, and today the building is a tire shop. The boom times lasted less than five years, yet this tiny dealership in a small Midwestern town had an impact that was felt from coast to coast.

Most race car interiors aren't this luxurious.

Yenko
Chevrolet

Canonsburg, Pennsylvania, Home of Perry Como and Don Yenko

While straight-line acceleration was the goal for most muscle-car folks, Don Yenko came from a background as a championship-winning road racer. His idea of "performance" included the ability to go around a corner without scraping the door handles off.

Located in Canonsburg, Pennsylvania, Yenko Chevrolet's name was seen on the side of the Corvettes that Don drove to good effect on race courses across America. His driving skill earned him the 1962 and 1963 SCCA B-Production National Championships, and soon people were coming to the dealership, looking to tap his knowledge for their cars. Yenko quickly saw that selling cars and parts that appealed to road-racing enthusiasts could put money in the coffers.

Ford's new Mustang was, once it had been massaged by Shelby American, kicking tail on the race track. Yenko saw the Corvair as the only Chevrolet vehicle that had a chance at beating the Shelby GT350s. With his racing background, Don was familiar with the Central Office Production Order system, allowing him to tailor a vehicle for a specific task and have it built at the factory. He order 100 1966 Corvair Corsas built with heavy-duty suspensions, M-21 four-speed manual transmissions, and special steering. He installed 3.89:1 Positraction differentials that he ordered over the counter along with dual master brake cylinders. Called Stingers, these Corvairs competed in D-Production, and in 1967, Jerry Thompson won the D-Production national championship in one.

Yenko believed that if you've got it, you should flaunt it. His cars had it, and they flaunted it.

Yenko Chevrolet built what became the best-known of the dealer specials.

Yenko continued to race while the dealership was wrenching on street performance machines. In 1967, Don Yenko and David Morgan captured first place in the GT category and 10th overall at the 12 Hours of Sebring race. That same year, the Camaro debuted. A General Motors edict stated that midsized vehicles were limited to engines with 400 cubic inches or less. Yenko quickly saw the Camaro as a potential basis for a serious performance car, but it needed more beans beneath the hood. Dana Chevrolet and Nickey Chevrolet had worked with Bill Thomas to stuff a 1966 Corvette 427-cubic-inch, 425-horsepower V-8 into a '67 Camaro, and Don Yenko tapped that knowledge by using Thomas as a source of performance equipment, such as headers and traction bars.

Yenko built 54 "Super Camaros" in 1967, all of them equipped with four-speed manual transmissions and dealer-installed complete 427-cubic-inch engines. Famed drag-racer Dick Harrell cherry-picked the components that were used the Yenko Super Camaros, such as the rear-end ratios, transmissions, exhaust systems, and clutches. Standard Camaro 350s would be shipped to Yenko's dealership, where the small-block would be pulled and a crate big-block would fill the space.

In order to maximize the number of vehicles that he could sell, Yenko concentrated considerable resources to create a nationwide distribution system. He had salesmen visit dealers with demonstrator Yenko vehicles, usually Camaros. He signed up dealers by giving them neck-stretching rides. Outfits such

transformation in one day. Sixty-eight 1968 Yenko Camaros were built.

Yenko started to really work the COPO system in 1969. He ordered Camaros as L78 396 cars, which meant Chevrolet would fit the cars with heavy-duty suspension components, bigger carburetors, and a 140-mph speedometer under the auspices of COPO #9737, the "Sports Car Conversion."

Under the hood, COPO #9561 was used, resulting in a 427-cubic-inch engine being fitted at the factory. The Rat powerplant could be bolted to either an M-22 four-speed manual tranny or a three-speed automatic. Buyers could choose to have the famous Yenko stripes deleted, but most wanted to flaunt what they had spent big bucks on. With the introduction of the COPO cars for 1969, the factory warranty was intact. That saved Yenko even more money.

Now that he had streamlined the process of having Camaros equipped with 427 engines built by the factory, he could move more cars. Production in 1969 resulted in 198 Camaros being "converted." Yenko turned his attention to a couple of other vehicles in the Chevrolet lineup, the Chevelle and Nova. It wasn't difficult to use the COPO system to have L-72 big-block engines installed in the Chevelle SS396. Only 99 were built, using the #9562 and #9737 COPO codes.

But try as he might, Don Yenko could not get Chevrolet to install the L-72 engine in the Nova. Something about liability. So his dealership had to pull the engine out of the stock Nova and slip the Corvette-based powerplant into the engine bay. The result was a car that Don Yenko described in an April 1987 *Muscle Car Review* magazine interview as "a beast . . . almost lethal. I was worried about that car; it was not for amateurs. I really was skirting the edge of product liability with that car."

as Chicago's Nickey Chevrolet and Los Angeles–based Dana Chevrolet were Yenko outlets.

To reduce costs, he ordered the 1968 cars with high-performance 396s. At the dealership, his crew would replace the 396 with a 427 short-block, meaning he would change out the block, pistons, and connecting rods and crankshaft. On top of the new parts, the original heads, intake manifold, and carburetor were installed. With fewer parts needing to be replaced, costs were reduced. The mechanics were paid $140 for each 427 Yenko Camaro they could complete. A technician working fast could finish the

As 1969 wound to a close, Don Yenko, like many others in the business, saw that upcoming regulations and tougher insurance rules would put a knife in the performance car market. So when the 1970 Yenko lineup was introduced, many were shocked by the absence of the Camaro and Chevelle. Only one car was being sold under the flag of performance, the Nova. By utilizing the COPO system again and checking #9010 and #9737 on the order form, the stock grocery-getter 350 normally found in a basic Nova was replaced with a solid-lifter LT-1 350/360-horsepower engine and the Sports Car Conversion package. The final product combined a lightweight platform with a potent, flexible engine, and the resulting $3,993 car sold well, to the tune of 175 units, making it the biggest-selling Yenko Super Car. Better yet, it was insurable as a "Nova 350."

As the 1970s marched on, it was clear that Chevrolet was out of the performance business, so Don Yenko took his business in new directions. By the mid-1980s, he owned a Subaru dealership and a Honda dealership. He was in negotiations with Jaguar and Hyundai about opening dealerships in the Pittsburgh when he was killed while landing his Cessna 210M at Charleston, West Virginia.

Yenko didn't just build Camaros. His first cars were Corvairs, and he built Yenko Super Car versions of just about every vehicle muscle car that Chevrolet produced.

Shelby
American

A Hybrid, on Steroids

Many get into the business of selling cars to get into racing, but Texan Carroll Shelby entered the world of selling vehicles after he had climbed to the top of sports car racing. In 1952, he won the first two races he competed in. His high-water mark as a driver was at the wheel of an Aston Martin DBR1, when he and co-driver Roy Salvadori won the 1959 24 Hours of Le Mans race.

Unknown to virtually everyone, Shelby was suffering from a heart aliment, angina pectoris, requiring him to slip nitroglycerine tablets under his tongue to keep the pain in check. He was using the medication while driving at Le Mans, but he refused to tell anyone for fear he would be yanked from the team. In 1960, the doctors told him that his driving career was over. But Shelby just shifted gears and moved into a new direction, with spectacular results. He wanted to run his own car company.

In 1962, Ford Motor Company had wrapped up development of a new lightweight V-8 engine displacing 221 cubic inches. Shelby, who knew people at Ford, got an engine and dropped it into an AC Ace, a small two-seat British sports car that was powered by a Bristol 2-liter straight-six. Shelby worked out an arrangement to bring engineless AC Aces to his shop in Los Angeles, California, where Ford small-block V-8s would be slipped in. The resulting car

Carroll Shelby: the man behind the legend.

Even back in the day, when everyone considered muscle cars disposable, everyone knew a Shelby Mustang was something special.

International Airport, leased from North American Aviation. These facilities would serve Shelby until Ford Motor Company decided in 1966 that it needed to exercise more control over the manufacturing process of the GT350 and the soon-to-come GT500. Carroll was, at the time, heavily involved in running Fords assault on the 24 Hours of Le Mans with a team of GT40s, and his attention was in France. Production of the GT350 and GT500 moved to Ionia, Michigan, where the cars would be built until production ceased in 1970.

In February 1968, former General Motors executive Semon E. "Bunkie" Knudsen arrived in Dearborn to take the reins at Ford. Because Shelby Cobras had humiliated Chevrolet on racetracks around the world, there was no love lost between Shelby and Knudsen. Knudsen initiated the Boss program at Ford, effectively killing the Shelby program.

After he was shown the door at Ford, Shelby moved to Chrysler, helping develop and market a line of front-drive small cars, such as the GLH. They didn't do much to fatten the corporate bottom line, but when Robert Lutz took charge of Chrysler, he approached Shelby about a two-seat sports car. The result was the Viper.

Shelby started his own company in Las Vegas, Nevada, building the two-seat, Oldsmobile-powered Series 1. In 2002, Shelby and Ford mended fences, and Shelby had a hand in the development of the Ford GT. With the introduction of a new Mustang in 2005, Shelby and the Mustang made history by once again building Shelby Mustangs, a partnership that lasted even after Shelby's death in 2012.

was called the Cobra. In no time, Cobras were kicking everyone's asses at racetracks across the country.

In April 1964, Ford introduced the Mustang, a cute, inexpensive, and not terribly fast vehicle. The Mustang sold well, but Ford approached Shelby with orders to transform the performance of the Mustang from adequate to thrilling. Carroll treated the Mustang to the same treatment as the AC Ace: inject more power beneath the hood, upgrade the suspension, then take it out to a race track. The result was the 1965 GT350. And like the Cobra, it was a dominant force on the track.

Business grew to the point that Shelby needed more production space, and he was able to move into two hangers on Imperial Highway at Los Angeles

5

Modern Muscle
Déjà Vu, Sort of

David Newhardt

It was both a celebration and a funeral. Chevrolet was celebrating the Camaro's 35th birthday in 2002, but the Camaro was dead. As early as 1996, it had been clear to the executives at General Motors that the Camaro was living on borrowed time. The F-body architecture was *very* long in the tooth, and GM just didn't have the desire or resources to create a new platform for a vehicle that was selling in relatively few numbers. So, like an old soldier, the Camaro was allowed to fade away. That was enough of a reason to pop corks in Dearborn. The Mustang was about to play in a field of one.

Ford Motor Company's biggest competitor to the Mustang might have exited stage right, but you'd never know it from the vehicles that used the Mustang as a starting point. The Fox platform that underpinned the Mustang was a robust, versatile assembly, and over the years it had been tweaked to

For 2008, Ford nipped a few bits from Ford Racing's parts department, like a fresh-air intake and a 3.73:1 rear differential gear set, and turned the already-quick Mustang GT into the Bullitt edition, named after Steve McQueen's character in the film of the same name.

To create the the Boss 302 version of the 2012 Mustang, Ford bumped output of the 5-liter Coyote V-8 by 32 horsepower, from 412 to 444, making it the most powerful normally aspirated Mustang ever produced.

within an inch of its life. Ford's internal performance division, Special Vehicle Team (SVT), had worked its magic on Mustangs over the years, including the 1984 SVO Mustang and the 2002 SVT Cobra. It was clear that performance continued to sell sporty cars.

The company kicked out limited-edition Mustangs as the millennium came and went, and the public's response to these cars made it clear to Ford executives that a successor to the Fox platform Mustang, SN95, would be a wise business move. Designer J Mays, in charge of Ford Styling, felt strongly that the next generation of Mustang had to look like a Mustang. In the early 2000s, there was a strong debate regarding the future configuration of the next iteration. One camp was in favor of retaining the front-engine/rear-drive setup, while some argued for a front-engine/front-wheel-drive vehicle. That latter car would become the Probe, as the outcry from Mustang enthusiasts was loud and clear when then heard that their beloved pony car might be front drive.

Dearborn planned to release the new Mustang for the 2005 model year, and it retained the iconic styling cues of the first generation 'Stang. A long-hood, short-deck stance was mandatory, as were tri-element taillights and a C-stamping in the side sheet metal. Equipped with either a 4.0-liter V-6 engine providing 210 horsepower or a 4.6-liter V-8 rated at 300 ponies,

the 2005 Mustang was a resounding success. How could it not be? Ford had the only pony car in town.

In 2001, Ford had introduced a special-edition model to honor the 1968 Mustang GT that Steve McQueen, as San Francisco police detective Frank Bullitt, drove in the movie *Bullitt*. Painted in Highland Green, it was a hit with buyers. Fast forward to 2008, and a Bullitt edition of the fifth-generation Mustang rolled onto the street. Packing a 4.6-liter V-8 with 315 horsepower and a five-speed manual transmission, the Bullitt could hit 60 miles per hour in 5 seconds, and the tightened-down suspension was ideal for chasing Chargers around the mean streets of San Fran.

For 2011, Ford slipped a new V-8 under the Mustang's hood, an all-new engine code-named Coyote. This 5.0-liter DOHC engine revived a famous

The 2016 Shelby GT350 didn't just redefine the Mustang; it redefined the entire genre of muscle car, blurring the distinction between the typical V-8-powered American brawler and the flat-out sports car. The 526-horsepower engine provided the brute force one expects in a muscle car, but the car's handling took it into another dimension of automotive experience

In case the driver forgot which version of the Challenger SRT8 he or she was driving, the "392" logos emblazoned in the upholstery were there as a reminder.

displacement from the prior millennium, but the new version was silky smooth, strong (412 horsepower), and efficient. And all this technology wasn't limited to just the standard Mustang GT; Ford brought a historic name back to the street in 2011 with the release

Dodge introduced the 392 version of the Challenger SRT8 for the 2011 model year. This version featured a punched-out Hemi V-8 that cranked out 470 horsepower. That's 20 horsepower more than the most powerful engine available during the classic muscle-car era: the 450-horsepower Chevrolet LS6

of the Boss 302. Under the hood, the Coyote 5.0-liter V-8 was tuned to generate 440 horsepower, and the car was available in two flavors: regular and Laguna Seca. The latter package is essentially a race-ready Mustang that *can* be driven on the street.

Blue Oval fans didn't have to wait forever for the next update to the Mustang; the sixth generation of the original pony car was released from the corral in July 2014 as a model-year '15. Various levels of performance were on tap, from a 300-horsepower V-6 to a 435-horse stormer. Equipped with an independent rear suspension, it had road-holding ability that could only have been dreamed of the year before.

Things got really serious in the 2016 model year, as the Shelby GT350 and GT350R were unveiled. With 526 ponies from their 5.2-liter flat-plane-crankshaft V-8, legitimate aerodynamic aids, and a suspension born on a race track, this was not a car for beginners.

Yet the War of the Ponies was just heating up. In the "classic" era of muscle cars, defined as the late 1960s to early 1970s, there was another corporation that built brutal machines—Chrysler. Since those halcyon days, Chrysler has undergone more ownership changes than you can count. In 1998, the company combined with German powerhouse Daimler, creating DaimlerChrysler, a so-called "merger of equals." While the supposed equality was clearly in favor of the Germans, Chrysler moved forward to re-enter the muscle-car field, and its LC platform was tapped to underpin a familiar name in muscle lore:the Dodge Challenger. Dodge was determined to retain the long-hood/short-deck proportions of the original 1970 Challenger, but the layout of the capable LC platform made this something of a challenge. The cowl couldn't be moved, and the driveline position was set. But the designers plowed ahead. While it was common knowledge that the car would eventually pack the 5.7-liter Hemi, the Challenger was first available for the 2008 model year in just one configuration—the 6.1-liter SRT8. Talk about coming out swinging!

Tired of being uncompetitive with the supercharged offerings from Ford and Chevrolet, Dodge pulled out all stops and introduced the 2015 Challenger SRT8 Hellcat. While this reverted to the 6.1-liter Hemi V-8 found in the standard SRT8 rather than the 6.4-liter version found in the 392, a supercharger pumped output up to 707 horsepower, making the Hellcat the most powerful muscle car ever built.

This 425-horsepower engine could vault the Challenger to 60 miles per hour in just a tick over 5 seconds.

Dodge released a new engine in 2003, a 5.7-liter third-generation Hemi, replacing the Magnum 5.9-liter engine found in Dodge pickups. This powerplant used an ingenious cylinder deactivation system that allowed the engine to run on four cylinders under light throttle, but when serious power was required, the engine instantly reactivated the cylinders that were loafing, resulting in all of the rated 375 horsepower when bolted to a six-speed manual transmission. This engine was slipped into the Challenger R/T's engine compartment starting in model year 2009.

In 2015 Dodge introduced the SRT Hellcat version of the Challenger. This car immediately vaulted to the pinnacle of all-time muscle-car performance thanks entirely to its powerplant: a 707-horsepower supercharged V-8. This environmentally unfriendly beast consumed so much fuel that the inner headlights had to be removed and replaced with additional air intakes to feed the hungry engine. While it was rated at 22 miles per gallon in highway driving, *Car and Driver* magazine managed just 13 in its testing, and a heavy right foot could drive that number down considerably more. Said right-foot efforts did result in a quarter-mile time of 11.7 seconds at 126 miles per hour, however.

But its crosstown rival in the Renaissance Center could read the tea leaves. Since the demise of the Camaro, General Motors had been besieged by bowtie enthusiasts clambering for its return. Behind the scenes at GM, a core group of hardcore car people were working tirelessly to bring back the fabled nameplate. Though the fifth-generation Camaro was conceived in 2004, the final product didn't roll into showrooms until the 2010 model was introduced in 2009, delayed in part because of the worst economic crisis since the Great Depression, which resulted in General Motors filing for bankruptcy. Chevrolet wanted to release both coupe and convertible versions at the same time, but the ragtop version didn't meet the expectations of the GM brass; rather than putting it on the market and using the public as beta testers, the suits held the introduction of the soft-top back one year while the bugs were worked out.

The top engine offering in the new Camaro was a 6.2-liter V-8, rated at 426 ponies when attached to a six-speed manual transmission. Like the Challenger, the Camaro was equipped with an independent rear suspension.

Next, Chevy released the brutal Camaro ZL1 in 2012. With 580 supercharged horsepower, this

For 2012, Chevrolet gave the fifth-generation Camaro a version of the 6.2-liter supercharged V-8 used in the Corvette. In Camaro trim, the engine cranked out 580 horsepower.

bruiser covered the quarter mile in 12.1 seconds at 117.4 miles per hour. And for 2013, the Camaro 1LE—a storied name at Chevrolet—hit the street. The intention of the original 1LE was a strong road-racing ability, and the 2013 edition follows in the same tracks. With many components "borrowed" from the ZL1, the 426-horsepower V-8 could carve a corner like a leech. Then, in the 2014 model year, Chevy released another classic nameplate from the vault: the Z28. With 500 horsepower and a full slate of racing-born equipment, this Camaro was essentially a full-blown track car with a license-plate frame.

For 2016, Chevrolet released yet another all-new rendition of the Camaro. Whereas the fifth-generation Camaro had been based on architecture borrowed from GM's Australian division, the sixth generation was based on the much more modern (and lighter) underpinnings of Cadillac's CTS and ATS models. As a result, the top SS model of the 2016 Camaro weighed 3,760 pounds, versus the 3,884-pound curb weight of the 2015 SS version.

The sixth-generation Camaro had more power pushing those fewer pounds, too. The top engine in 2016 was the new 1LT V-8 sourced from the Corvette, which pumps out 455 horsepower at 6,000 rpm and 455 pounds-feet of torque at 4,400 rpm.

For 2017, Chevrolet brought back both the ZL1 and the 1LE package, the top-dog ZL1 once again featuring a supercharged 6.2-liter V-8 cranking out 650 horsepower and 650 pounds-feet of torque. The Z28 seems destined to once again reappear for the 2018 model year, and rumors have that model being powered by either the ZL1 engine or a 505-horsepower, normally aspirated 7-liter V-8.

To borrow a saying from Mark Twain, the reports of muscle cars' death have been greatly exaggerated. They have been repeatedly threatened with extinction over the years, yet they come back stronger than ever. To tree huggers, the loud, vibrant muscle car is an easy target as a symbol for all that's wrong with automobiles. But today's cars are environmentally friendly, safe, and fun, and—unlike most of the rolling dreck clogging the roads—they make a personal statement.

You want the rarest of the rare? How about one of one 1967 Shelby GT500 Super Snakes. Carroll Shelby built this 520-horsepower car for a high-speed tire test. It sold for $3,000,000 at auction in 2008. Today the price is somewhere north of if-you-have-to-ask...

My favorite Camaro of all time: the 1968 Z/28 convertible. This is the only first-generation convertible Z/28 Camaro ever built. Built by GM for Pete Estes specifically to get him to sign off on racing options for the 1969 model year, this British Racing Green convertible may look harmless, but it is all business underneath, with Cross Ram dual quads, fiberglass hood, close-ratio four-speed, JL8 four-wheel disc brakes, and other items GM needed to get into production to beat the Fords in SCCA competition. A wicked way to get a tan! *Sam Murtaugh, courtesy of Mecum Auction, Inc.*

Blue-Chip Muscle

Colin Comer

6

In folklore, there is a formula known as the cosmogonic cycle. A character must endure this cycle before becoming a hero. While the formula varies depending on the storyteller, the basic principle is the same: unremarkable (or at least unheroic) characters go through stages on their journeys to test their mettle, rising to something greater than they were before. Generally, the cycle begins with a call to adventure, followed by an entry into the great unknown. The unknown reveals a series of difficult trials, physical impediments, and mental and moral ultimatums, until an ultimate test returns the protagonist to the real world as a hero. If there were ever a mythological parallel to the journey of muscle cars through time, the cosmogonic cycle is it. These bright, shiny machines entered the world as socially acceptable, as innocent as the youth market to which they were aimed, only to be thrashed within inches of their lives and later viewed as undesirable cars driven by undesirable owners. The machines that survived with enough redeeming qualities to be rescued and restored were then thrust back into the limelight, once again shiny and socially acceptable—not to mention more valuable than ever!

Face it—muscle cars were never intended to be valuable. In fact, the whole idea behind muscle cars was that they were inexpensive and fast. Muscle cars were stripped-down versions of the most utilitarian, homely, and basic mass-produced cars ever to roll out of Detroit—rattle-trap, bare-bone crude devices built to conform to a price point with little regard given to sophistication or longevity. These were the cars every red-blooded American kid wanted. The image, the speed, and the lifestyle were all highly addictive. Looking back, the muscle car years were a relatively brief moment in time that we will never see the likes of again. It was a perfect storm, just what the market wanted, and was presented at the right place in the right time.

So after many years of being "just old cars," how did these seemingly disposable machines, built in large numbers, owned by kids who literally tried to kill them from the first twist of the key, become so

167

valuable? More importantly, why did they become so valuable? Where is the inherent value in blue-chip muscle cars, and why are people willing to pay so dearly for them?

Stepping back and looking at the collector-car world as a whole, a few distinct trends are evident. Seasoned collectors recite certain maxims that are the hallmarks of inherent value. The most common is performance, regardless of the era of the vehicle. One can arguably break the most valuable collector cars down into three distinct categories: pre-war full classics and competition cars; post-war sports and competition cars; and American muscle cars. The one thing they all have in common is that they were ahead of their time in performance, whether it be a Duesenberg SJ, a pontoon-fendered 1958

Ferrari Testarossa, or a Super Duty Pontiac. These types of cars were limited production, competition-proven cars in their day, and revolutionary at the time. While muscle cars are a distinctly American phenomenon, those who think they do not have the same inherent Ferrari-like value gained through racing are sadly mistaken. In European road racing, only the ultra-wealthy independents or factory teams had the means to become truly successful. The average enthusiast was stuck on the sidelines watching and never dreamed of being involved. But drag racing and factory-built muscle changed all of that. The average guy could go to a dealership and, armed with the right information, buy a car from the factory, go racing, and win. The age-old saying of "Win on Sunday, sell on Monday" is very true. Drag racing

Another blue-chip Shelby with no roof, this 1969 GT500 convertible in Grabber Orange—one of 335 produced—marked an end of an era. All 1969 and 1970 Shelbys were built in 1969; unsold units were re-tagged and sold as 1970 model year cars. It was an interesting end to a very interesting era, to be sure! *Sam Murtaugh, courtesy of Mecum Auction, Inc.*

Perhaps the wildest supercars ever built were Joel Rosen's Baldwin-Motion cars. This 1970-1/2 B-M Phase III 454 Camaro, owned by Les Quam, is proof of that. At an original price of over $6,000 out the door, Rosen guaranteed this Phase III Camaro would cover the quarter mile in under 12 seconds. Turns out it was actually capable of 11.6 seconds, right out of the box. Now that's one potent supercar! Today, real documented B-M cars such as this one cost a hell of a lot more than $6,000. *Paul Zazzarine, courtesy of the Les Quam Collection*

made competition attainable for the average guy and sold cars. Outside of drag racing, another American phenomenon was taking hold—NASCAR. The early days of stock-car racing also fueled the fire for consumers who wanted factory-built muscle.

What all this amounts to is that the inherent, core values for the most sought-after collectible cars are basically the same. They were all the best of their kind, all emphasized performance, and all were proven in competition. Where muscle cars excel is the fact that they were obtainable or at least viewed as such. A new Duesenberg SJ was not an obtainable goal for most, nor was it the best in road racing or sports-car racing. In the United States, few could relate to these exotic cars (even if they could afford

them). So the youth market was primed for an affordable, attainable performance car they could use. The muscle-car era was the ultimate incarnation of these factors. Value was born from a delicate blend of rarity, provenance, condition, and history—along with a heavy dose of nostalgia.

It came as no surprise when the muscle-car era wheezed to a stop in 1973. From government regulations involving pollution control and safety to insurance companies reluctant to insure high-performance cars, another perfect storm occurred—one that nailed the coffin shut on muscle cars. For most, it was no big loss. But for those who loved performance, it was a sad conclusion to something they hoped would never end. As every following year brought less

Is there a more sinister-looking muscle car than a black-on-black 1970 Hemi 'Cuda? Compared with their convertible stablemates, these 426 Hemi hardtops provide all the bang for a lot less buck. Sure, they built 652 of them, but that still qualifies as rare in my book, especially if you go for one of the 284 four-speed cars in rare colors like this one. This 16,000-mile former award winner sold for $270,000 in 2009, representing about an 80 percent discount over the convertible version. *Sam Murtaugh, courtesy of Mecum Auction, Inc.*

and less performance from Detroit's latest offerings, many people started seeking out used muscle from the glory days of 1964–1972. It was the beginning of the muscle-car collecting hobby, whether they knew it or not!

As performance vehicles began to disappear from showrooms, savvy dealerships, owners and collectors started saving the best muscle cars. They also sought out the special cars. By the late 1970s, supply and demand kicked in, and some ultra-rare cars, such as Boss 429 Mustangs, Hemi Mopars, Yenkos, and other supercars, were appreciating rapidly. Keep in mind that "rapidly" is relative to the values of the cars. When a $4,000 car appreciates to $6,000, that is a 50 percent jump and quite impressive. By the 1980s, there was a real industry in place that supplied parts for people restoring these cars. And the more prices kept appreciating, the more cars started to come to the surface and be saved. Most muscle-car

enthusiasts saved and restored the vehicles not for the potential investment value but for a simpler reason: they loved the vehicles. What's more, the potential monetary return wasn't all that great, considering the time, effort, and cost involved. But those who recognized the importance of rare muscle cars early on and had the foresight to buy and maintain them certainly were proven right in the long run. Looking back to the 1980s, I remember watching this new breed of collectors buying muscle cars from the old-line gearheads who were still thrashing them as well as digging out great cars from long-term owners. When I saw a friend pay $2,500 for a faded yet amazingly nice 1965 GTO Tri-Power four-speed hardtop and get ridiculed by friends because he could have had a 1977 Trans Am instead, I was shocked—the GTO seemed way cooler, but then again, I was just a kid on the sidelines. Some other examples of great finds when the prices started to appreciate during that time were the 1973 SD Trans Am for $1,500 (needed work, but all there); the one-owner 1971 442 W-30 convertible for $4,000; and an absolutely mint 1970 Boss 429 I watched sell in 1989 for $5,700 after a bidding war broke out on the owner's front lawn.

What started as a slow escalation of prices had suddenly gained momentum, but it was nothing compared to what happened next. In 1987, Otis Chandler, *LA Times* publisher and legendary collector of significant cars and motorcycles, also recognized the significance of important muscle cars. He enlisted Greg Joseph to help him make a list of the most significant muscle cars ever built. When the list was completed, they went shopping. As soon as the word got out as to what was going on, prices started to jump like they never had before, but more importantly, Chandler basically legitimized the importance of rare muscle to non-muscle car collectors. Suddenly it was OK to have a Hemi 'Cuda sitting next to your Duesenberg. Not that people ran out and bought them, but at least they felt justified in doing so.

As the cars gained momentum in the market, buyers needed to know if what they were buying were not only truly rare, but also truly genuine. Experts and enthusiasts compiled information gleaned from factory literature and production records and noted the numbers and nuances of the actual cars. The more the cars appreciated, the more people were willing to pay for this extra layer of insurance, which in turn gave birth to another industry within the industry—that of VIN and trim tag decoding books all the way to professionals for hire to inspect the cars for buyers. Of course, as some people learned about numbers, others doctored them, putting those numbers where they shouldn't have been, such as on non-original engines, or even worse, making bogus VINs or trim tags, essentially creating cars that didn't exist. Just like anywhere else money flows into, the crooks ride in along with it.

Despite the best efforts of these crooks, great (and real) cars still appreciated rapidly. Within a few short years in the mid-1990s, the cars that had already doubled or even quadrupled in price did it yet again. Muscle cars worth $200,000 were starting to appear common, and soon reports surfaced of some ultra-rare cars approaching the million-dollar mark. It wasn't long before that milestone was surpassed as well. Most people are astounded when they hear that some muscle cars have sold for over a million dollars; to the uninitiated, a muscle car selling for over a million dollars is like seeing a unicorn jumping over a rainbow. Nevertheless, out of the hundreds of thousands of muscle cars built, there are a handful of examples worthy of this price level.

This is a good place to explore one particular type of blue-chip muscle car; in fact, it's probably the poster child for the whole muscle car value rocket

Sporting the highest horsepower rating of any car during the muscle-car era, the 1970 LS6 Chevelles claimed 450 horsepower from their mean 454-cubic-inch engines. Thanks to relatively high production numbers, examples like this well-documented Fathom Blue hardtop are logically valued in the low-$100,000 range today. A virtual high-water mark in the horsepower wars, these will always be highly sought-after machines. *Sam Murtaugh, courtesy of Mecum Auction, Inc.*

Early muscle doesn't get much better than the Super Duty Pontiacs. They literally dominated Super Stock drag racing with cars like this factory lightweight 1963 421 Super Duty Catalina. Sporting factory-installed aluminum front fenders, hoods, bumpers, and other lightweight components, they stand as a testament to the lengths manufacturers will go to win on Sunday and sell on Monday! *Sam Murtaugh, courtesy of Mecum Auction, Inc.*

ship ride of the last decade or so: Mopar Hemi E-Body convertibles. These 1970 and 1971 Hemi 'Cuda and Hemi Challenger drop-tops are the undisputed kings of the two-comma muscle car club. Let's look at the timeline. When these cars were new, nobody wanted one (as Joe Oldham makes clear earlier in this book). Well, almost nobody—to be more precise, between both cars and both 1970 and 1971 model years, a grand total of 41 Hemi E-Body convertibles were sold.

Worldwide.

This was a result of the Street Hemi's reputation for being a finicky beast, the high cost of the option, and the fact that nobody who truly wanted to go fast wanted a convertible. So what made these cars undesirable when new has now made them ultra-desirable simply because Chrysler hardly built any. How's that for revenge? But the sum of the parts makes sense as well. They are the wildest and best-looking motors to ever leave any American auto factory, are the best-looking cars Chrysler ever built, and have tops that go down. There isn't another 425-horsepower convertible pony car from this era. They have the legend, they have the look, and they have the mystique. And that 41-built number makes them as rare as politicians with common sense.

It was a beguiling turnaround—within ten years of the end of their original production, a time when no one wanted them, people sought these cars and were even willing to pay a premium price for them. By the late 1970s, they cost roughly $10,000. In the mid-1980s, they had gone to the mid-$20k range. By the late 1980s, a good Hemi 'Cuda convertible

Speaking of Super Duty Pontiacs, this one-of-six 1961 Pontiac Tempest 421 Super Duty coupe is beyond rare. A purpose-built race car, it also has an all-aluminum front end and something even crazier out back: a four-speed transaxle! Out of the six built, only two of these cars remain. *Sam Murtaugh, courtesy of Mecum Auction, Inc.*

More rare Pontiac muscle: This 1968 Firebird with the little-known Ram Air 1 engine is one of 413 produced. Rated conservatively at 335 horsepower and 430 lb-ft of torque, this L67 code 400-cubic-inch engine offers a ton of motivation for the little Firebird. *Sam Murtaugh, courtesy of Mecum Auction, Inc.*

sold just into six-figure territory. Another ten years down the line, they were around a quarter of a million bucks. In December 1999, headline news was made when a 1971 Hemi 'Cuda convertible seized by police in a Washington State drug bust was sold at auction for $410,000. By 2001 or 2002, Hemi convertibles became serious commodities, with a few 1971 'Cuda convertibles changing hands in the $500,000–$750,000 range.

Then something happened that really pulled the pin. In late 2002, collector Milton Robson of Atlanta placed a huge ad in *Hemmings Motor News* for his one-of-two 1971 Hemi 'Cuda four-speed convertible, a car he had owned since 1988. Milton had a few lines about the car, with the price in big, bold type for all to see: $1,000,000. One million bucks. For a Mopar. While these cars had been trading for money close to Milton's seven-figure price, they were all private sales and not public knowledge. But this ad in the bible of the hobby changed all that. Milton sold his car for $1,000,000.00. The car bounced around a little before ending up with a well-known Mopar collector in Illinois. In September of 2003, CNN published an article on million-dollar muscle cars being a reality. On the cover of the December 2003 *Mopar Action* magazine, Milton's old car was featured with the headline "$1,000,000 'CUDA—The Inside Story." Big dollar muscle was big news.

Once the ball was rolling, Hemi 'Cuda convertible prices took off running. While every sales result since the late 1970s had doubled the prior one, these cars were at such substantial dollar amounts that this doubling was serious. Wild reports of multi-million-dollar sales became the norm. Twelve months after their last million-dollar headline, the December 2004 *Mopar Action* featured a white 1971 Hemi 'Cuda convertible on their cover with the headline, "WORLD'S MOST VALUABLE MUSCLECAR! $2 MILLION HEMICUDA." The feature car was the last Hemi 'Cuda convertible built and one of the two export models produced, having been originally sold in France.

It had recently passed through the hands of a few well-known Mopar collectors, the last in England, who sold it to a Hemi ragtop collector in Arizona. In September 2005, this owner reportedly turned down a $4.1-million bid for this car at auction. Another sale of a 1971 'Cuda convertible was reported in 2005 at $3 million. In January 2006, a 1970 Hemi 'Cuda convertible sold at the Barrett-Jackson auction for $2,160,000. Numerous news reports of these sales and related values were published, seeing print in such mainstream publications as the *New York Times*, *USA Today*, *CNN*, and many others.

While this unprecedented jump in Hemi E-Body convertible values remained headline news, they weren't the only cars in the two-comma club. By 2006, there were enough million-dollar-plus sales for me to write *Million Dollar Muscle Cars*, a book published in 2007. Some of these million-plus cars were the aforementioned Hemi E-Body convertibles but the list also included cars such as the 1969 ZL-1 Camaros, 1969 Trans-Am convertibles, the one-of-one 1968 Camaro Z/28 convertible, and the one-of-one 1967 Shelby GT500 Super Snake. But so fast-paced was the market at the time that I also included a number of chapters on cars that were six figures and rising. This list included Ram Air IV GTO convertibles, 1969 Dodge Hemi Daytonas, 1970 Chevelle LS6 convertibles, and other ultra-rare muscle cars.

The first-ever big-block Chevelles were the 1965 SS 396 cars. Internally known as R.P.O. (Regular Production Option) Z16, the 201 examples produced are now just known as Z16s. These were really special machines, with upgraded frames, suspension, brakes, and of course that famous 375-horsepower, L37-code big-block 396. Unlike stripped-down muscle, the Z16 cars had certain mandatory options such as AM/FM radios, seat belts, and padded dashboards. If you like big-block Chevelles, thank the guys who pushed for the Z16 option and got it into production, since these are the cars that started it all. *Sam Murtaugh, courtesy of Mecum Auction, Inc.*

The last section of the book dealt with alternatives to mega-dollar muscle, and I encouraged readers to seek out cars that had the same hallmark of value of more expensive examples: low production. These were unique muscle cars with great appeal that somehow stayed under the radar. Sleepers, in other words. These, to me, are far more desirable than a lot of cars that snuck into the big-buck party with a forged invitation. For example, just because an LS6 Chevelle

convertible was worth $750,000, a 350 Malibu convertible with a crate 454 engine dropped in it and $500 of SS badges and stripes is not worth $100,000. I watched as people snapped up these imposters thinking it was the only way to get a cool muscle car, and I fully understood the desire but not the logic. But it is often hard for people to apply logic in purely emotional purchases. This whole period of rapidly escalating prices, fueled by headlines, televised, high-profile auctions, and a "now or never" feeding frenzy was epic. Even the most mundane muscle cars were bringing prices that the blue-chip cars had struggled to achieve five years prior. And let's not talk about restomods, "tribute" or clone cars, and the like. They all fall under the guests-with-forged-invitations

Right below the one-of-one 1968 Z/28 in the pecking order of coolest first-gen F-Body convertibles are the eight (yes, eight) 1969 Pontiac Trans Am convertibles. Although you'll rarely, if ever, see one publically for sale, fully expect a two-comma price tag attached if you do. While they don't have an exotic engine like the 426 Hemi-powered 'Cuda and Challenger drop-tops, one-of-eight says it all. And the 1969 Trans Am is pretty damn cool to begin with. *Sam Murtaugh, courtesy of Mecum Auction, Inc*

The 1969/1970 Ford Mustang Boss 429 cars are some of the most outrageous pony cars to ever leave Dearborn. So outrageous was stuffing Ford's NASCAR-bred Boss 429 engine into the little Mustang that Ford actually subcontracted the deal to Michigan's Kar Kraft because the modifications and effort needed far exceeded what Ford could accomplish on its assembly line. While the real-world performance of the Boss 429s never quite measured up, nobody can say a Boss 429 isn't badass. Just look at this 1969 version: simple and understated, with that now-famous stance and ginormous hood scoop that says it all. *Colin Comer*

Ace Wilson's Royal Pontiac was to Pontiac guys what Yenko and Baldwin Performance were to Chevy guys. If you owned a GTO, the only thing better was to have a "Royal Bobcat" fortified one. Beyond selling Bobcat hop-up kits over the counter and even doing in-house Bobcat conversions, Royal would also do more invasive procedures. One example is this Royal-converted 1968 GTO supercar known as the "BossMan." When new, it was fitted with a 428-cubic-inch engine at Royal. The conversion was immortalized with an in-process photo featured on the cover of *Popular Hot Rodding* in March 1968, showing Royal's Milt Shornack and Dave Warren dropping in the 428. It is that kind of documented history that adds great value today. *Sam Murtaugh, courtesy of Mecum Auction, Inc.*

DODGE ANNOUNCES SCAT CITY
The '70 Dodge Scat Pack is road ready.

Scat City is anywhere competition is hot, keen, and sanctioned.

It's the day after race day . . . U.S.A.! In a small brick building in Highland Park, Michigan, a group of white-coated engineers roll a long-snooted automobile into a closed van. In the Daytona Beach airport, NASCAR winner Bobby Isaacs catches a plane for Chelsea, Michigan . . . proving ground for the Scat Pack Chargers. Monday morning

at 5 a.m., the "Wing Thing," the new Charger Daytona, goes for a shakedown run . . . flat out.

"Big Daddy" Don Garlits, king of the dragsters, hot from shutting down two dozen fuelies at a Long Island rail meet, catches a cab for Kennedy Airport. His destination—Michigan International Speedway and a date with the hot new Dodge Challenger R/T. Daddy digs it. See report inside.

From the USAC wars, former national champion Don White wings in to blast the 1970 Charger R/T around the high-bank Michigan circuit. His opinion . . . "A great muscle car for all-purpose driving . . . and it's even got a functional back seat."

Up the river, the guys in the parts department are stuffing boxes with speed goodies . . . selected intakes, jugs, cams, cranks, mags, headers . . . the works for the guys who won't take stock for an answer. Special show kits for those who want special styling.

California Charlie Allen, the all-American boy, world's greatest Dodge Dart drag race artist, shows up to smoke the new version of the Swinger 340. At

Detroit Dragway the budget bomb lives up to its name.

Dandy Dick Landy, who races for loot, puts his boot in the new Super Bee SixPack. Finds out it sizzles and gets off the line like lightning.

Scat City is where it's taking place, where the Dodge Scat Pack cars are proving to be the toughest performance cars going. From Riverside to Race-

way Park . . . from Dallas drags to super speedways. And back at the shop, a group is putting the finishing touches on a thing called the Scat Pack Club. Yes, gang, you do have a friend at the factory . . . he's waiting to talk to you.

Welcome to Scat City—where the competition is hot, hairy, and sanctioned. Be a swinger and join the Scat Pack Club. Details on the following pages. And don't forget . . . keep the tach in the black!

heading. As they say, a rising tide hoists all ships, and there were many examples of this in the great value charge of 2004–2006.

Nobody knew where the tide would take us. Of course, the safe money would be on what goes *up* must come *down*, but really it was anybody's guess. In *Million Dollar Muscle Cars*, I summed up the market as follows:

So where are the values heading? Logic would tell us that the unprecedented appreciation in such a short time is not sustainable with these cars. As with anything, supply and demand will dictate values. Only time, the owners, and the prospective buyers will set the stage for what comes next. Regardless of what happens, it is guaranteed to be as exciting to watch as it has been for the last twenty years.

What nobody accurately predicted at the time was the global financial crisis of 2008 that we are still in today (this is, without question, the largest factor in muscle-car values post-2006). The worst financial crisis since the Great Depression has been pretty effective at slamming the brakes on purchases of expensive play toys like muscle cars, not to mention real estate, the stock market, and financial institutions. Values of all collector cars tumbled, and muscle cars were right at the forefront. In many cases, it is hard to say exactly to what extent values dropped, as many of the higher-priced cars just couldn't find buyers. The owners who had to sell, and unfortunately there were many, learned the hard way that the market wasn't what it was. As quickly as many cars doubled in value, they de-valued even quicker, especially cars that didn't deserve high valuations in the first place, such as clone and tribute cars.

Cars like our poster child Hemi E-Body convertibles didn't become worthless by any means— 'Cuda convertibles still stayed above that magical $1,000,000 mark famously set in 2002—but they certainly were not multi-million-dollar cars anymore. Probably the worst-hit segment of the muscle-car market was Mopar muscle cars in general. Is it because they were the ones that appreciated the most? Probably. Regardless, it's another example of when leading the charge isn't always a good thing.

Tracking the market since 2008 has been interesting, to say the least. That year became a very quiet year, bringing with it the obvious change from a seller's market to a buyer's market. Buyers now had ample time to research and think about prospective purchases and a newfound power to negotiate. Owners with great cars that they didn't have to sell wisely sat on them and monitored the market. Many of the fly-by-night collector car dealers and brokers

that filled the market like paintless dent repair guys after a hailstorm folded up shop and moved on to greener pastures. Many auction companies, quick to acknowledge that owners were no longer comfortable with the no-reserve auction format in this catch-a-falling-knife environment, again allowed reserve prices on cars at auction. Like any market, once the shock wore off and people got back to business, cars started trading hands again at "new" prices. This activity helped buyers get a handle on the new market once values stabilized. And on the best of cars, indeed they did. By late 2009, the great cars were moving again, and prices were appreciating for the first time since 2008.

Slowly but surely, our key blue-chip cars were selling again. Buyers, sensing opportunity, sought the best of the best. While Mopar muscle cars have not rebounded well at all, most other high-level cars have. The laws of supply and demand have kicked in again as well; now that the mandatory fire-sale cars are off the market and buyers again have to search for that rare car, sellers have a little leverage. If you lust for a numbers-matching, original paint, four-speed 1969 Yenko Camaro, and should you actually *find* one, be prepared to pay what it takes to own it. It is still as significant as it was before the Great Recession, and it can still be had today at a discount—not a bad deal in my book.

Another factor driving the market is the question of where else in this perhaps fatally wounded economy do people feel safe putting their hard-earned money? The Bernie Madoffs of the world have made it abundantly clear that tangible goods are not always bad to own. So while the market may not always be great or exceed what you paid for a blue-chip muscle

car, there will always be a buyer somewhere ready to write you a check. That's an awfully reassuring thought compared to the uncertainty of paper investments. Plus, I've never seen anybody doing a smoky burnout with a stock portfolio, but maybe I just missed it.

Perhaps the single biggest change from the heady days of four-million-dollar Hemi 'Cuda convertibles in 2006 to today is that the buyers are different. When muscle cars first took off in value in the 1980s, people who really wanted them could still chase them and buy them if they had to—after all, the guy who was going to pay $30,000 for a Hemi 'Cuda could most likely pay $40,000 if he really had to own it. But when the cars jumped to huge numbers and never came back down, there was a certain

Pontiac built the GTO Judge for three years, during which they made 293 Judge convertibles. Total. That fact alone puts them on the blue-chip list. Plus, they are freaking cool. This 1970 Atoll Blue version sold for $350,000 in 2009, not only because it's one of just 168 1970 Judge convertibles built but also because it is one of less than 20 with the big dog Ram Air IV engine. It may seem expensive, but this is one exclusive club.

My favorite GTO? I'm pretty fond of my 1965 convertible. It has the Tri-Power 389, close-ratio four-speed, a 3.90:1 rear, and nothing else. No heater, no radio—heck, it barely even has hubcaps. Cars like this don't cost a ton of dough, and they will always have a strong following, just as they have since they were new. GTO folks are a loyal bunch, which bodes well for future collectability.

The 1965 Shelby GT 350 may be more sports car than muscle car, but I've never met a muscle-car guy who didn't love it. With 521 produced, these first-year Shelby Mustangs are as solid a bet as you can make in collector cars. And if you drive one, it will take a month to get the stupid grin off your face. These cars were hardly affected at all during the 2008–2009 dip in the market and have had an incredibly stable upward value curve for the last 25 years. That says a lot.

segment of buyers who just decided it wasn't worth it. The guys who drove these cars when they were just cool old cars largely didn't see the fun in treating them as priceless objects of garage art. One could argue that this scenario has repeated itself numerous times within the muscle-car market over the last thirty years as new money comes in and prices out the old market.

Which brings me, finally, to the most positive result of the Great Recession value dropout: it shook a lot of non-car-guy investors out, and the resultant period of lower prices and flat appreciation curve, as short as it was, drew end users back in. Guys who wanted that Yenko Camaro they lusted after as a teenager but couldn't justify buying, let along using, one

at 2006 prices, could now justify both. In *Million-Dollar Muscle Cars* I wrote:

> It's a shame many of today's buyers won't get to experience these cars the way we could when they were relatively inexpensive. Not many people will take their Hemi 'Cuda and drive it to the grocery store, or enter into an impromptu street battle. Now you have to worry about hurting an original engine or mortally wounding a nearly priceless collectable, which is a shame because using these cars is where the fun is. Living with a muscle car and learning its qualities (or lack thereof) are what endeared them to people in the first place.

Thankfully, this seems to be changing. It is wonderful to see people using these cars as (gasp!) cars

If the slab-sided styling of the 1964–1965 GTOs doesn't resonate with you, how about the famous Coke-bottle 1966–1967 models? This is a 1967 fitted with the famous Hurst mag wheels.

Another flavor of GTO Judge Convertible: a 1969 Ram Air III, one of only 108 produced.

again. The venues in which like-minded owners can get together and exercise muscle cars keep growing. Everything from weekly local cruise nights to thousand-mile road rallies to events like the Supercar Reunion offer owners a chance to see what their cars (and themselves, in some cases) are made of. This activity feeds itself by encouraging non-owners to start thinking about finally buying the car they have always wanted. As awful as this global financial collapse has been, it is encouraging to see that blue-chip muscle has weathered the storm exceptionally well and is again appreciating. To the naysayers, the pre-2007 market was a house of cards, ready to crumble at any moment and leave people with virtually worthless cars that nobody would ever buy. To see it emerge as healthy as it is certainly proves more than a few people recognize the significance of the cars in question.

The good news is that the values that have and remain to be realized by the most rare and significant muscle cars will preserve them for future generations, as well as save many from extinction. High values make it sensible to rescue and properly restore

rare cars rather than let them rust into oblivion or be "restored" with cost as the main inhibiting criteria, rather than making them correct and doing a proper restoration, which by definition entails bringing something back to new condition, flaws and all. If we didn't have this strong upward trend in pricing over the last few decades, most muscle car "restorations" would still consist of rattle cans of spray paint and undercoating, chrome Moroso valve covers, and a new set of air shocks.

One of the biggest movements in the collector-car world today (including muscle cars) is that of preservation-level, unrestored original cars. These time-capsule examples, which are few and far between, not only offer a reference point to show us exactly how to restore cars that are no longer original but also show us that restoring great original cars erases real history. For any car to survive 40 or 50 years without any restorative efforts is amazing, even more so when it is a muscle car. So small was the number of muscle cars that were bought but not used as intended, or cut up and raced, that it should come

Yenko built more than just Camaro aupercars. In 1969, he built just 99 Yenko 427 Chevelles. This LeMans Blue example is among the best. Low in mileage and still sporting original paint, it has the winning combination of rarity and originality. *Sam Murtaugh, courtesy Mecum Auction, Inc.*

Did you think I was kidding about using these cars? At the Supercar Reunion in 2008, I had no problem drag racing my concours-restored 1968 Yenko Super Camaro against Dru Diesner in his very fast 1969 Yenko Super Camaro. These are cars, after all, and a great part of the enjoyment of owning them comes from actually using them. *Colin Comer*

as no surprise that a truly spectacular unrestored one can be worth several times more than a comparable restored example. If you ask my opinion on the best bet for future appreciation in blue-chip muscle, it is to find the best lowest-production, highest-horsepower, documented, and completely unrestored car you can. Proof of just how important it is to recognize original unrestored cars can be seen in the all-makes SURVIVOR car show held every June in conjunction with the Bloomington Gold Corvette show. So if you find an untouched '65 GTO in a Southern California garage still owned by the little old lady who bought it new, snap it up and don't touch it!

So what can be gained by looking back at the last forty years of muscle car values with perfect 20/20 hindsight? Quite a bit. Like our fictional folklore character, the best muscle cars fell from grace when they became "just used cars," then slowly but surely they escaped the seedy underworld, met the challenges and physical impediments thrown at

them, and were able to return to the world of collectibles as heroes. While the plot may have ups and downs along the way, the overall trajectory is clearly upward. To survive insurance blacklisting, gas crises, generational shifts, world economic meltdown, and still come out spinning their tires is impressive. I certainly can't predict the future any better than I could in 2006, but using historical data as a guide, I'd say the future looks rosy for the finest blue-chip muscle cars. After all, the 1964–1971 era of muscle cars is really the last era of truly collectible American cars. Much like the full classics that preceded them, I think we'll be seeing a lot more of these babies in the years to come. What more can we ask for than that?

PHOTO CREDITS

All photos by David Newhardt except the following:

Dave Anderson: pages 10, 12, 13, 14.

Randy Leffingwell: pages 36, 37, 38, 39 (bottom right), 41, 42, 43, 45 (top), 47, 48 (bottom), 53, 56, 59 (bottom), 60 (top), 61, 62, 63.

Joe Oldham: pages 69, 70 (bottom), 75, 76, 77, 78, 79, 81, 82, 83, 85, 86 (top), 88, 91, 92, 93, 98, 99 (top), 100, 103, 104, 106, 107 (bottom), 108, 109, 113, 114, 117, 118, 119.

Sam Murtaugh, Courtesy of Mecum's Auctions Inc.: pages 166 (bottom), 168, 170, 172, 173, 174, 175, 176, 177 (bottom).

Colin Comer: pages 177 (top), 185 (bottom), 186.

Courtesy of Shelby American, Inc.: page 179.

John Hollansworth, Jr., Courtesy of Mecum's Auctions Inc.: page 180.

INDEX

AUTHOR BIOS

Jim Wangers

Jim Wangers, the legendary Pontiac ad man, created the mystique that surrounds America's original muscle car, the Pontiac GTO. Wangers conceived many of the best-known marketing programs of the muscle-car era. The author of *Glory Days*, the 84-years-young Wangers lives in Oceanside, California.

Joe Oldham

Joe Oldham, who tested (i.e., street raced) muscle cars for several top magazines back in the day, is the author of *Muscle Car Confidential*, a tell-all behind-the-scenes look at how these cars earned their performance numbers, giving a firsthand sense of what it was like to live in the muscle car era.

Colin Comer

Few people are as passionate about cars as Colin Comer. After spending the better part of two decades building a successful restoration business and collector car dealership, Comer found another passion in life: writing. A contributing editor to *Sports Car Market* magazine since 2004, Comer has authored three award-winning books for Motorbooks: *Million-Dollar Muscle Cars* (2007), *The Complete Book of Shelby Automobiles* (2009), and *Shelby Cobra: Fifty Years* (2011).

Randy Leffingwell

Randy Leffingwell, best-selling MBI author and top-notch photographer, has earned a reputation as one of the most thorough Corvette historians working today. He has written and photographed over two dozen books on topics ranging from tractors to motorcycles to cars to barns.

David Newhardt

David Newhardt is one of the best automobile photographers working today. He is the author of such best-selling books as *American Muscle Supercars: Ultimate Street Performance from Shelby, Baldwin-Motion, Mr. Norm and Other Legendary Tuners*, *Complete Book of Camaro*, *Art of the Muscle Car*, and *Pontiac Firebird Trans Am*, and has provided photography for *GTO: Pontiac's Great One*, *Camaro: Five Generations of Performance*, *Muscle: America's Legendary Performance Cars*, *Corvette Fifty Years*, *Mustang Forty Years*, *Mopar Muscle*, *Shelby Mustang: Racer for the Street*, *Camaro Forty Years*, and many more.

Darwin Holmstrom

Darwin Holmstrom has written or co-written many books on muscle cars, including the best-selling *Camaro: Five Generations of Speed*, *GTO: Pontiac's Great One*, *Hemi Muscle Cars*, *Camaro: Forty Years*, and *Muscle: America's Legendary Performance Cars*.